HURRY WALTER, THERE IS A POSSUM IN THE HEN HOUSE

WHAT A MESS DOWN ON THE FARM

CRICKET WEBB

HURRY WALTER, THERE IS A POSSUM IN THE HEN HOUSE WHAT A MESS DOWN ON THE FARM

iUniverse books may be ordered through booksellers or by contacting:

iUniverse
1663 Liberty Drive
Bloomington, IN 47403
www.iuniverse.com
1-800-Authors (1-800-288-4677)

ISBN: 978-1-5320-9561-0 (sc)
ISBN: 978-1-5320-9533-7 (e)

Library of Congress Control Number: 2020903926

Print information available on the last page.

iUniverse rev. date: 02/29/2020

INTRODUCTION

Thank you for purchasing this book! I think you will enjoy reading about our family's life as crazy as it is at times. It is the truth that there are days we are high functioning and slightly normal family, but it is seldom that this does happen.

As I wrote this book, I can tell you that every story contained herein is the truth, while some family members will try to deny that it ever really happened. I was there most of the time for the events in this book, and some at the time may not have seemed so funny, but as the years have passed and we look back, the stories have become so much more laughable.

I can tell you with this book you may not laugh at every page, but hopefully, it will bring a smile to your face and remind you of a time in your life.

Some of the names in the book have been changed, and it was not because they were innocent, while others are just who they are in every day of their life.

I want to thank my parents, who brought me up with a good sense of humor, to always be honest, love God and Country, and your family as did my special Aunt and Uncle. I want to thank my daughter, her husband, and three grandsons for giving me so much material to use. Their life is everyday drama, so there are always stories of some kind coming out of their front door.

I want to thank Rents Everett, who encouraged me on everything I worried about and told me it would all work out because God was with me. Rents knows how I love to make others laugh.

I want to include this dedication to my beloved brother, Lee, who left us much too early in 1978, and who we miss every day. Lee, I always feel your presence.

To my paternal grandfather, William Graddy Webb, who always said to me, "Laugh and the World laughs with you, Cry, and you will Cry Alone."

While there may be some words that look like they are misspelled, they are not; they have merely been spelled the way we country folk talk sometimes or the way the children were pronouncing their words. Even though we have a college education when you are on the farm, the country slang sucks you right in with it.

COMING HOME

As a teenager, I could not wait to get off the dead-end road, where I had grown up and experience life. I moved to the big city, after High School to further my education, and I was happy that I accomplished all that I had set out to do so far.

I remember dating a boy that my mother knew, and I had never met, and the first time he came to my house to pick me up for our date. Oh, my goodness. I would die of embarrassment. My Dad and an uncle were outside neutering a tomcat. You heard me right; that is what country folk do that have no money. The new feller said hi to them, and what are you doing there? Dad says, neutering a tomcat. Dad pointed the scalpel at my date and said, "This is what happens to any guy who steps out of line around here." I dug a hole, crawled into it, and pulled the grass back over me. I was sure my dating life was over.

When Lee and I were fairly young, Mom would take us with her while she picked wild blackberries. It so happened that while she was picking the wild blackberries, my brother and I were playing in an old mud hole, the tractors had rutted out pretty deep in a slough. My brother and I only had two TV stations to watch out in the country, and we saw plenty of westerns. We knew all about that quicksand stuff and how dangerous it was for anybody who walked off into it. Lee got to playing around the edge of that mudhole and slipped in, and sure enough, it was quicksand right here in the bootheel of Missouri! He kept sinking deeper and deeper and started telling me it was quicksand. I screamed for Momma. She never came to help so it was up to me to get him out, so I did what they did in the movies and ran to get a long broken off tree limb. He grabbed it, and I was finally able to pull him to safety. I was frightened so badly it made my knees weak.

My momma, my dad's mom, my brother Lee, and I were all in the back yard, snapping green beans under a plum tree. Naturally, being the honery older sister, I was trying to tell on my brother for everything he was doing because he was not helping snap that horrible pile of beans we had to get done. The first thing he did was drink like a dog out of the green water of the dog bowl. At the time, I just wanted Momma to make him stop, today it gags me thinking about it.

I was snapping away on the green beans as had been instructed listening to my mom and grandma talk, when all of a sudden, the green bean I picked up did not feel like the others. I looked down, and it was a green garden snake about twelve inches long that had fallen out of the tree into my pan. I screamed a real girl scream, a blood-curdling scream, and threw the big pan of about a gallon of freshly snapped green beans to hither regions of the back yard, and I have no idea of what happened to the snake. I shouldn't have been scared of the snake as it was harmless, but at that moment, it might as well have been a spitting cobra.

At the age of six, I learned a very valuable lesson in life, and that was never sass your mother if she has her hands in dishwater. She will slap you with a wet soapy hand every time, and this causes an added sting. Well, Ms. Stubborn went back in for another dose. I sassed her again. I saw she was going to chase me to whoop me, so I took off, tearing out the front door. Wrong door, I had to run barefooted through all those fresh sweet gum balls that had fallen from the tree. It slowed me down enough; she caught up with me and I got my whoopin. Note to self: when sassin your mother make sure she is not doing dishes and her hands are dry, plan escape route before sassing and make sure you have on good running shoes.

But, it didn't take me long to see all that 'life' had to offer in the big city, and I wanted desperately to come back to the quiet complacency that the dead-end road had to offer that was still familiar from the years of my growing up in the country. I would have never believed it of myself. I guess you really can't take the country out of the girl.

I was so happy to be back on the family farm with its familiar sights, smells, and two of the people I loved more than the world itself, my parents. Both very positive people in my young years and still that way today, and I could always depend on them being there for me. They were what I called "real parents." They were the kind of parents that most kids dream of having.

Oh, we had our 'head-buttins' as we called them, about whether I should do this or that, but they were not bad, they were the mild disagreements that teenagers have with their parents. The kind that soon blows over and the kind when you grow up, you reCocoaze how smart your parents had become since you moved away from home. I had only been moved for about two weeks, and my parents I.Q. had risen about 100 points from what I thought it had been. After I had my daughter, my parent's IQ raised another hundred points. My parents were MENSA class folks.

There was so much always happening on that dead-end road. Life was never dull. Between my father and I, my poor mother, never knew what to expect next. Seriously, she never knew when the next phone call to go to the Emergency Room would be. It was always "cray-cray," to say the least.

But, my mom was a real pioneer woman, not afraid of much of anything. One day while she was babysitting my daughter and keeping my little dog "Polly" who was half dachshund, half shitzu, mom could hear Polly barking out by the pump house, and she could tell that Polly was furious. Mom looked out the kitchen window overlooking the yard and saw her in a furious battle with a groundhog that was much larger than little Polly herself.

Mom was worried about Polly's life, so she ran outside, grabbed a shovel, and without thinking as small as Mom was, she welded that shovel above her head and came flat down on the groundhogs head – SPLAT! Killed that groundhog deader than a doorknob, I tell you it is the truth! Mollie grabbed that groundhog-like she had killed it herself, shaking it like nothing you have ever seen! How in the world a little dog could shake a groundhog that big was a shocker to me. Mom sat the shovel down and came back into the house. Her job was finished; she had saved Mollie's life. I heard all about it when I got home from work. I was proud of her for that little execution of the groundhog if it was about to get my Polly girl. Polly was Gabby's personal 24/7 babysitter.

When it came time to put Gabby in school, I decided it was to be a private Christian School. You know, a learn at your own pace, no drugs, no one acting out of line and good kids attending. Well, let me tell you something that hit this Momma in the face and sent her into a tailspin.

I picked her up from school one day, and while driving home, things were going great, and she was chattering like always. She never shut up, and I heard everything every day. She suddenly turned to me at seven years old and said, "Momma, what is a virgin?" Oh, Lord, where had she heard that word? I went off the pavement and threw rocks everywhere, thought I was going to lose control of the SUV and was shaking all over. I pulled to the side of the road and tried to compose myself before turning to look at her. I asked in what I thought was a very calm voice that inside my mind was screaming, who is the person that said that word????? Instead, I said, "Honey who said that word to you?" She told me that Mikey down at the stump on the playground said I was probably still a virgin. I told her, "Well, you are and that is the way you want to stay for a long, long time, and when the time comes, we will talk more about it." She said, ok.

I took a big deep breath and pulled back on the highway when she said, "But what does it mean?" If that little boy was here right now, I could do serious damage to his body parts. Again I regained my composure even though I had thrown up in the back of my mouth, and I was choking on it and had started to cough. Man, that makes your throat burn. How disgusting is that taste? I explained that shortly, I would buy a book, and we would sit down, and I would explain the definition of a virgin

to her so she could understand it much better. Would that be
ok? For now, concentrate on having fun and do not hang around
Mikey ever again and stay away from the stump.

The very next day, she gets in the SUV, and we are talking
about school, and she is singing away. She stops and says, "Guess
what Mikey wanted all us girls to do down at the stump today?"
I asked, "You were with Mikey again today?" I felt the vomit
coming up in my throat again. I was going to have to stop eating
lunch every day and only drink water in the afternoon. She
responded, "Yeah, we were all down there first, and he came
down to the stump." Lord, help me with whatever Mikey did
today. Please help me from committing a felony. Gabby went on
to say, "He wanted all us girls to lift our blouses." I know my
smile was so fake, and I could not change the position of my
smile. I asked her when they wouldn't do it what Mikey said.
She said he kept asking till the bell rung.

I thought things with Mikey were about to calm down
when I noticed one morning after seeing some books she had
left in the car, so I ran them back into her. Mikey sat across the
aisle from her!!!!!! That struck fear in my heart for sure. I looked
at him with a look that could have pulverized him into black
smoke. But he was still sitting there when I did my double-take.

I told the teacher (one who I liked) that there were a few
problems with Mikey and went over the issues down by the
'stump' on the playground. I mean, come on people. That boy
at seven already had a one-track mind. Where did all that
testosterone come from at that age? Why was I paying all this
money for this boy to be stalking my daughter?

I then went on to tell the teacher that he had been feeling up Gabby's pantyhose and was going pretty high, and if it did not stop, I was going to chop off both of his hands and the one thing that he seemed to be becoming so fond.

After this talk, all talks of Mikey ceased. Our conversations soon moved on to the birthday parties of her and her friends. Those, while boring, were much better than those we had been having on Mikey.

One afternoon, when I dropped by to pick my always cheerful daughter up, one of her teachers stopped me and said, "I just have to tell you what happened at lunch today." When it starts like that, you immediately go over scenarios in your mind. The teacher continued that Gabby had brought her lunch, and she prayed for about ten minutes over her lunch sack. Finally, the teacher asked Gabby if everything was okay, and Gabby told her she had been praying and praying that those fish sticks in her bag would taste better after she prayed, but nothing had changed. They still tasted nasty.

We never have any idea what will happen each day when we wake up, such as the day that the skunk was walking across the field during the middle of the day in front of our house. That just was not 'real' normal in our part of the country. They were usually night time critters. So, my dad and his friend decided to check it out. I told my daughter to grab the movie camera and film it. She questioned the fact, but Mom and I assured her to stay in the opposite direction of the wind, and everything would be fine. She put on a pair of rubber boots that went up to her knees, and she took off with her long red hair flying in the wind.

The guys were already bent over the stump where the "hole" was at where they thought the skunk had gone in to hide. Gabby had positioned herself to video just right to capture what was about to happen. The guys told her where it would be safe for her to stand to tape the good stuff.

All of a sudden, the trapped skunk came running out so they could make sure it was healthy and not rabid as so many were that year. If rabid, the guys knew what would have to be done. Dad and his friend started to shake the old stump. <u>Nothing</u>! They rocked it a lot harder the next time. The skunk came out long enough to spray, and it all went in the direction of the camera girl.

I had stayed at home on the porch with my mother watching from afar. Gabby came stomping back across the field. I could tell by her walk that she was angry, but from where we were, we had no inkling as to what had taken place. The boots were too large for Gabby, so it made her stomping look a little odd like she had a limp, but it was a stomp, no doubt.

When she got to the edge of our front yard, we began to smell her or rather the skunk perfume, and when Gabby stomped onto the porch, we could smell her new scent very well. It had sprayed her good. It was on her clothes and in all that beautiful red hair. She was livid and almost acting rabid herself. With redheads, you know how that is. She looked at mom and me and said that she never knew why in the world she ever listened to either of us. Every time she did, something stupid happened to her. She should have known better. She stomped off into the house for a shower and to change clothes. It took several days to get the skunk smell entirely out of her hair and our house. Her clothes, oh my, they went into the laundry by themselves. As for the guys, the wind was not blowing their direction, and they didn't get any skunk smell on them whatsoever.

I remember the day Gabby decided she wanted to buy a rabbit for a pet. Relentlessly we tried to talk her out of it. She tirelessly would not give up on asking the same thing over and over. She was buying it with her own money and had to pay for everything for it. We bought the rabbit at a pet store in St. Louis. The pet store put the rabbit in a cardboard box that boldly had printed on the side that, at one time, it had carried "Kotex" in it. She would not take the box to the car. She was so mortified; that this was the box she had been bestowed with to carry her new beloved pet home. She bought a collar, a leash, and purchased everything a pampered rabbit could want in its life. The rabbit was solid white.

The entire 180 miles home was discussing what she should name the rabbit. Finally, she decided she would name her new rabbit Itsy Bitsy and call her Bitsy. We stopped in a town close to our home and purchased Bitsy, a new cage. Gabby did not plan on having her in her cage that much; but, just in case we were to be gone, Bitsy could stay in the cage for her safety. Yeah, for whoever wants to believe that story.

Bitsy settled into her life at her new home quickly. She fit in as if she had always lived there, it seemed. WOW, did she grow fast? Gabby would take her for walks on her leash, and one morning while walking her in the vegetable garden, one of our domesticated cats, Maxi, decided he was going to have Bitsy for lunch. He jumped on her, startled Gabby so bad that she screamed. Next thing we knew, Bitsy was being swung above Gabby's head at the end of the leash and going round and round like a ceiling fan blade. Poor Bitsy, she would soon be choked to death. I ran to Bitsy's rescue, knowing she could not take much of that as rabbits go into shock quickly. Gabby got her beloved rabbit, and they went into the house. I can assure you there were no more long walks outside with Bitsy.

Bitsy had quite a ravenous appetite. She chomped rabbit mouth marks all along each side of our treadmill, chewed the ear clip to keep up with your heart rate into two pieces. Ate an antique linen tablecloth, a large dried flower arrangement, and chewed a telephone cord in two pieces. The Rabbit-Goat went on to eat a welcome mat (yes, I said an entire rug welcome mat with the rubber backing), ate a flowering pocket plant to the soil, and ate the screen out of a new screen in a window (this was a real feat as she did not escape after eating her way to freedom).

One day, we were sitting on our screened-in porch and swinging, and Gabby decided she was going to hold Bitsy. Bitsy, being Bitsy, chose to make Gabby chase her. Bitsy ran to the corner where an old hard guitar case was standing in the corner, and Bitsy was like magic! She ran right through the guitar case! Gabby turned to me and said, "Did you just see what I saw?" I replied, "Yes, I believe I did. That was weird." It was one of the old 1950s hard guitar cases bear in mind. Gabby went slowly over to the guitar case, afraid of what it might behold, and gradually picked up the guitar case and turned it around. Oh, MY GOODNESS!! That rabbit had chewed out the whole backside of the guitar case!!! No wonder she could run through it! She was no rabbit; she was a goat.

Being as we were making Gabby pay for the destruction of what her Bitsy was up to, Gabby was running out of money pretty quick. She had paid for a rabbit, for rabbit food, for a collar, a leash, a water bottle, all the luxuries for a rabbit.

Gabby came into the kitchen one morning and said that she needed to find a home for Bitsy as she could not afford her anymore as she was 'eating her out of our home.' I agreed, and a friend of mine at work, Jacee, gladly took her off our hands to put with her pet rabbits. When we got to Jacee's house, we found out Bitsy was never a Bitsy, but a BENNY!

The VERY next day, while leaving for work, Gabby's step-dad came back home within minutes after leaving, and what did he walk into the house with? A black and white tamed rabbit, a huge tamed rabbit! The rabbit had been sitting smack dab in the middle of the highway as he turned off our county road. What was going on? Gabby immediately said it was not going to be her rabbit. Get it a home somewhere right now. So, poor Jacee got another call.

Gabby and her step-brother decided they wanted to get a pair of hamsters together. They had a habit trail already, and why not each purchase a hamster? They were so happy to have a couple of hamsters. They named them Lizzy and Bubba, and they were going to let them have children and sell them back to the pet store and get rich. OK, if you say so.

The first two nights, Bubba and Lizzy ran on the wheel all night long. The third night, they tore up paper all night long. They kept Gabby's step-brother awake most of the night. It was so stinkin funny. The hamsters were gotten out at night, and Gabby and her brother would play with and talk to their hamsters.

Then one Saturday morning, Bubba and Lizzy were not in the Habi-Trail! Everyone was searching high and low. Where had they gone? It was going to be cold weather soon, and if they didn't find them before long, they might freeze! The wide search turned up nothing. They had only had them for a couple of sleepless weeks! What could a parent say about that?

The hunting ceased, and we decided to keep an eye out for them, and if they got hungry, they would show back up, maybe. Maybe this had turned into a cadaver recovery. The day went on uneventful. Gabby got the rainbow vacuum cleaner out that afternoon for me and was going to put water in its tank, and she screamed her head off. When she took the top off, there was Lizzy! No Bubba, but there was Lizzy. I think Lizzy went to live with Gabby's cousins, and the Habit Trail did too.

My little Polly dog was getting old, and her heart and liver were failing. Her body's organ systems were not supporting her little brain anymore. The desires were still there, but the body could not follow through. She had been such a protector for Gabby from day one when Gabby was brought home from the hospital. That dog made such a mark on our lives that when I get to the Pearly Gates, I hope she is there waiting for me so I can hug her over and over again, and she can lick my face with joy. She brought pure happiness to all who met her all the years she lived.

She was Gabby's nanny. If Gabby wet her diaper, even a little, Polly would get me and bark and then go back to Gabby's side and sit there. When we first brought Gabby home from the hospital, I was feeding her, because she wanted to eat all the time. It was exhausting. I did not know then that Lupus haunted my health, and that could have explained the pure exhaustion and my need for deep sleep.

Gabby's cries sounded like a tiny kitten mewing and were barely audible. Not to Polly, she slept by her bassinet and any little whimper; Polly would wake me up by coming to my side of the bed and barking for me to check on the baby. Her baby! The little drill sergeant she was would make sure I was taking care of her the right way.

As Gabby got older and started walking, Polly was right beside her; all the time. When Gabby was swinging on her swing set outside, Polly would sit under the glider, and it would just brush across the top of Polly's head and brush her fur.

If Gabby would take off where Polly did not think she should be going, then Polly would get hold of her pants legs or whatever she could get hold of and drag her back to where she belonged. Polly was a busy dog when Gabby started walking. You never saw one without the other.

If Gabby had to stand in the corner for something, Polly stood in the corner with her. Only Polly would turn and look at me like I was the meanest person in the world. Gee, I wouldn't make her stand there for more than 2 or 3 minutes at a time.

Dad loved all things outdoors and all kinds of hunting and fishing equipment at one time. When he got his license to hunt with a crossbow, he was so excited when he got the new bow home he decided to see how it would feel to shoot it. One bad problem: he did not read the directions as he had always told my brother and me that we should do. He prepared his crossbow to shoot it in the master bedroom. Lord have mercy. You are not supposed to dryfire a crossbow. When he pulled the trigger, the string went crazy, came off, and slapped Dad across the face and even hit him in the eye. He was like an old cat that had something hot thrown in its face.

He wanted whatever was making his eyes hurt to stop and stop right that minute. He kept rubbing his eyes and trying to figure out if he would ever see again. Had he blinded himself with that crossbow the first thing? He sure hoped not. And his face, he had not looked in the mirror but was pretty sure it had sliced his face wide open. That is going to need stitches, but of course, he could not see, but he could not feel it bleeding. What in the world had he done? Was this a permanent injury, and he would be blind forever, and he would never be able to hunt again? Mom came into the bedroom where he had decided to conduct his first experiment and looked the injury over. For sure there were red whelps but she could find no permanent damage per his eyes that were visible. His vision, well, they would have to wait till the morning and see if he still had any vision. Men and their toys and not reading directions.

I never knew my mom loved chickens so much until my oldest grandson, Bobby Lee, and his class had an incubator, and they were hatching baby chicks. It was a cool second-grade project and a HUGE deal for him. He got so involved in this project that he told the teacher that his grandma and grandpa lived on a farm, and they might take the chicks. At first, it was going to be to watch after two of them during Easter break, and then it wound up being to take in six and make them a home, and that meant homes forever.

I do not know what happened to my mother; I guess the same thing that happens to me when I get a new baby possum. I go crazy and start planning for the whole brood. The next thing I knew, she had my Dad take her out to buy one of those wood buildings that are on skids that were shaped like a barn and had a little loft in it with a front door that looked like a barn door. She went and bought even more baby chicks. She and Dad were putting up a fence. Then they added another window to the little barn and a sliding window that looked like a sliding door down next to the floor with a ramp that went outside so the chickens could go in and out the sliding door.

The next thing I knew, there was a chicken calendar, three large framed pictures of handsome hunks of roosters, a chicken clock, and mom even put curtains up in the chicken house windows. Next, there was a radio placed in the chicken house to play country music. In the summer, they had fans blowing on them; in the winter, there were water warmers so their water would not freeze. Mom called them her girls. None of them ever had to worry about growing old and going into the cooking pot. When they got old, they lived out their days there in the chicken yard giving other hens advice and just clucking around until they went to that big chicken yard in the sky. They lived in the perfect chicken world. Couldn't ask for better than that.

Then came the summer of the duck. That summer, Mom had wound up with someone's leftover duck from Easter. When the duck got pretty big, he still thought he was a chicken because he had always been around other chickens. He never recognized he was a duck until he came to live in Mom's chicken yard when she gave him his first swimming pool. He loved the swimming pool. He would sit in it for hours, and his chicken friends that he had grown up with would stand around the pool, wondering why he wanted to stay in the water all the time. He would quack away and swim forever. He was so happy with this new toy. Of course, his name was not hard; it was plain ole 'Duck.' No point in it being awkward. He was the only duck, so keep it simple.

It was almost winter and Mom could not decide how she was going to take care of Duck all winter and keep his pool from freezing, and he couldn't go to roost at night; he was going to freeze. He needed other duck friends, and he needed them quick. So, she and dad took Duck and turned him loose at a Lake north of a local city. I could not sleep worrying about him. He did not have any friends there. He knew no other duck friends. I was having great difficulty coping with how Duck would adapt. So, when I would get off work, I would drive out to where Duck had been turned loose and look for him. I could not be for sure, but for a couple of days, I thought I saw him, and he was alone and staying off to himself. The third day I went out to the lake, I saw who I thought was Duck and a lady friend. If that was him, he now had someone. I felt better and would not let myself go back. I had to let it go, and in my mind, I had to tell myself that Duck was better off in the best place any duck could be where he could live out his life with all the ducks that lived on that blissful but protected duck paradise.

While I love all things possum, my Mother and I have the opposite affection for them. Any possum I could find, I am always trying to save them so they could live out their life to its fullest. Mom, on the other hand, has some inborn anger against the same creatures as she is sure they are getting into her henhouse at night and eating her hens. I cannot believe that. Possums are the Lord's clean-up crew, and I have never known a possum to kill something to eat it. Possums are valuable as they can eat up to 4,000 ticks a day. I think that is very important, especially where we live.

One particular morning mom found a possum in the hen house, no dead chicken anywhere, but the possum was curled up in a chicken nest and in a deep slumber. Mom smacked him on the head with Dad's tactical flashlight and grabbed him by the tail and carried him outside to a cage of some sort, and dropped him in the cage, not even gently. Seriously? Is that any way to wake up any of God's creatures? Was there no empathy whatsoever? I am sure the little thing had a headache as it had never had before! We discussed the flashlight smacking.

Mom stomped into the house (Dad said he could hear her stomping up the ramp to the back door) threw open the rear French doors and told Dad the sordid details and all about her anger at the possum. It was now his responsibility to haul said possum away, far away from her chicken house so he would never return. He could eat ticks somewhere else on the farm.

Dad said to her in his slow southern drawl, "Well, momma, I wish you wouldn't have used my good flashlight to be hitting them possums on their heads." Mom stomped off with Dad's flashlight still gripped tightly in her hand.

Later that morning, Dad went out to visit the possum in the cage and was trying to decipher the best action he could take so they would know for sure this possum did not show up back in Mom's chicken yard. He looked around and found a can of purple spray paint. Dad picked it up, and spray painted said possum real good with the purple paint. He noticed that mom had messed up the hair on the possum's scalp when she hit him. Dad felt sorry for the old possum. He loaded the purple possum in his side by side, and off they went for a ride out to the woods a couple of miles from Mom's grasp.

There were more possums sprayed purple that summer in our county than there was probably in the entire world than you could ever think about. I am sure when people would see the purple possums, they would look two or three times to see if their eyes were working right. I mean a purple possum in the woods??? How crazy is that?

It seemed every morning for a while when Mom went to the henhouse; there was some new disaster causing major drama. Some morning's there would be a dead chicken inside the henhouse. But they could never figure out what was getting in through the doors and killing the chickens. She always screamed; **it was a possum.** Come on, always blaming the possums! Don't think about fox, coyote, mink, rats, the list goes on and on of the eligible varmints that could do the dirty deed. I still felt it had to be an inside job myself. But, Mom kept blaming the possums. Dad kept checking the perimeters for ways for predators to get under or over the fences and any footprints by critters. But there was never anything like you would expect.

One morning when Mom went into the henhouse there, as big as life was, a huge chicken snake curled up in one of the chicken's nest. Mom was livid...AGAIN! Dad was inside in his recliner. He could hear Mom stomping up the back ramp, AGAIN onto the sun porch as she stormed into the house. He lay there thinking any minute she would be stomping in the dining room French doors, and he would hear about the latest fiasco. She said, "Hurry Walter, Get your gun, there's a snake curled up in my chicken's nest, and I think he is full of my eggs!" Dad, being married 61 years to this woman, did as he had been ordered to do. He got his pistol, and outside, he went where Momma had stormed back out to what had become the "highway of the danger zone."

When Dad arrived on the 'scene,' the snake, the very long snake might I add, was picked up from his sleeping pose in the nest with a garden hoe. Dad picked him up by the tail and flung him out in the chicken yard. Dad, while standing in the chicken house doorway with Mom standing right behind her man not wanting to miss one detail, saw Dad aim at the snake with the pistol, and 'BOOM' blasted that big ole chicken snake in two pieces. For his age he was still an excellent shot. Mom could not hear a thing for an hour or two because the blast was right in her ears. She wore hearing aids, so I am sure the explosion was double magnified by her standing inside the chicken house behind the blast. It caused the snake to throw up some of the eggs he had swallowed, and then Bogie, the old yellow lab, and who I might add had been designated as the "World's Greatest Hunting Dog" grabbed the snake and gave him a good shake, which caused more eggs to eject from the snake's mouth. Mom was furious at all the eggs he had eaten. She was fit to be tied.

When Mom gets angry, the angry does not leave quickly. Dad has learned he either leans back in his recliner and pretends to be sleeping or semi leans back and looks like he is reading the paper. Or if her mad is terrible, he will go to his shop and pretend to work on something. I can tell you that he has been working on the same old lawn mower for over five years. Mom has not figured that out yet and that is best. It is Dad's secret getaway.

One evening late, right at dark thirty, I ran over to Mom and Dad's house to get something, but what it was I cannot remember and have not been able to ever recall. Why I cannot remember I think is because when I got to the bottom of their handicap ramp, Dad was standing there in his cotton knit pajama shorts, a green tank top, rubber boots up to his knees, a boonie hat, and holding a live animal trap in one hand and his tactical flashlight in the other. He looked so funny I could not imagine what he was doing at this time at dusk outside in the mosquitoes. I asked him, "Where in the world are you going, or is this a new fashion statement?"

He said in his slow southern drawl, "Yore momma is mad. She says the armadillers are eatin' up her sweet taters, and I have to catch the armadiller and get rid of him." I asked him if he had seen the tracks, or was he going on her word? He said, "I am just going out there and doing what she told me to do. I have been married to this woman for over 60 years, and this is the best thing for me to do right now so I can get some sleep." I said, "Isn't it your bedtime?" He replied, "Yep, I was ready for bed when I got these instructions. That is why I am wearin these clothes." I forgot what I went after, and I was giggling so hard I just went back home. Besides, if mom was on a tear about an armadillo, I didn't want in the middle of it.

There are some things in your life you wish you could go back and erase but are never able to get rid of, and there are some people who will never let you forget specific experiences in your life and will continue to remind you of those most embarrassing moments for as long as they can remember them and that is usually until they get dementia.

I am the first to admit that I am a very naïve person. But, let me explain, I was raised on a dead-end road, did not know you could buy meat, or pickles from a store till I was a teenager. We lived 26 miles from a town of about 18,000 and only went there once a month, and sometimes it was much longer. The only people besides ourselves we ever saw were the mailman and my grandpa that lived down the road from us.

The most embarrassing moment of my life did not happen at the actual time it happened, but the day after. I was a Director, where I worked and was at the Annual Awards Banquet sitting at the head table with the HR Director, the CNO, and her husband, the CEO, the CFO, and I cannot remember if there was anyone else. I am so glad that I cannot remember anyone else. I never blush, but this story still gets to me this day. I laugh about it, and it is funny, but I still cannot believe how naïve I was at that time and probably still am.

We started discussing all kinds of things, and somehow the subject came up that I cooked wild game. They asked me what kind of wild game I did cook. I told them venison, duck, turkey, goose, and when I was lucky enough to get one, I cooked Beaver.

They all looked at me kinda odd and said, "You cook your Beaver?" I thought this was a strange question, but answered honestly and told them yes, my family loves Beaver. It tastes like Beef, and some say even Elk. I could not, of course, stop there but went on to say, "Dr. Pauly has had my Beaver, and he loves it! When he has had my beaver, I usually make a warm gravy to put over it, and then you can eat it over warmed buns. He said if he were not already married, he would marry me for my beaver."

By then the whole table was laughing, some were laughing so hard they were crying. My CEO had tears running down his face, and his face was blood red. The Chief Financial Officer, who never smiled about anything, was laughing till he was crying. The HR Director looked at me and said, "You might want to stop talking now." I said, "Am I saying something I shouldn't? Is there someone here that belongs to PETA?" She said, "No, but you might want to change the subject." I couldn't figure out why they all kept laughing now, and then they would ask me a question which at the time I did not realize was a loaded question, and I answered as sincerely as I could because I was serious as I could be about the topic. They would look at me and break out in laughter for the rest of the evening.

The next day at work, the HR Director came into my office, and I was not thinking a thing about it as she dropped by pretty often to discuss different issues with me. She said, "About last night, I thought I might let you know what everyone was laughing about." I said, "Yeah, why was that so funny? I never knew what the deal was. Were some of the PETA people there or something?" The HR Director said, "Not exactly, it is just that Beaver can mean something else besides the animal sometimes." I had a very blank look on my face, I guess. She said, "You don't have any idea, do you?" I told her I had no idea to what she was referring. She went on to explain that 'beaver' had sexual innuendos that I had NEVER heard of in my life! She went on to explain. My embarrassment then was so terrible, being naïve can sure get you in a hot mess.

How had I never heard of this? I will tell you why! I had my nose so buried in books all these years and was never a party person and so darned naïve. There were probably a lot of other words that I might be saying that was bad too. It was time to round the troops of my step kids and my daughter and her husband; they were going to give me an in-service. How dare they keep me in the dark and let me make a fool of myself in a public place!

Needless to say, that every time someone new started working at the hospital, the Beaver subject came up, and everyone wanted to know the story. I know for sure when the CEO I served under at that time; is ever old, and in a nursing home somewhere, he will remember that story, and the staff will have no idea what he is talking and laughing about and think he is out of his mind. But he will be in his right mind, and he will be recalling something that made him laugh so hard that he could not quit laughing and had tears streaming down his face.

I will remember what happened because I was so naïve that I had no idea that what I was talking about was making me look like a fool until the next day. It made me wish I never had to come out of my office again or that I had a Halloween mask to wear when I went out into the halls. I talk way too much and say what is on my mind. If it is there, it just comes out, no filter sometimes. I never intend to hurt anyone; I am just brutally honest.

And yes, I am naïve, still, but I kind of like being naïve at times. It can be an ugly world if we think about it. I like looking at it through rose-colored glasses! I love to have my glass always half full. One thing I do know about with this experience, even with me being naïve, I have given a few people something to look back on and laugh about on a dreary day.

Dad loved to go to the Lake to troll and fish for crappie.
He could sit for hours, trolling and jigging for the next big
one. When I went with him, I would fall asleep so quickly. The
rocking of the boat going back and forth. In the spring, when
the crappie would be biting, the trees of all kinds would be
blooming, and bloom was floating in the air.

Dad usually had mom with him on these adventures if it
was her day off, but today was not one of them. He was at the
Lake, and all the bloom in the air was makin him sneeze a LOT.
Before he knew it, a BIG sneeze hit him something terrible, and
he sneezed his entire set of false teeth right out into that lake. He
watched them, and they floated down into the depths of the clear
water. Oh my, Momma was a going to be mad about him losing
his teeth. That was not something he could hide when he went
home. Even if he didn't grin, she would notice the difference
right away.

He was right, and she was MAD!! He did not say anything
much to her. She scolded him as to why he had not put his teeth
into his pocket and button it if he was sneezing so bad. He
said, "Well, Momma, I was enjoying being out there fishing so
much I never gave it another thought until I saw them sinking
in the water and it was too late to put them in my pocket." For
a long time after that, friends and family who knew what had
happened to his teeth would tease him that they saw a great big
bass at the lake wearing someone's false teeth.

When I moved to the big city 3 hours away to finish my
schooling, I had no idea what a car alarm was as I had never
heard of such a thing. I have never smoked marijuana and had
never wanted to, nor had I ever drank liquor as that was not
the direction I had chosen for my life. I was a severe Geek. I
liked school, and I loved learning. It seemed like there were not

enough things to learn as fast as I wanted to learn them, and that may have been part of my problem.

I will never forget the day in Biology Class when a girl named Kayla was working on an assignment while we were all in the classroom, and we had the windows open because it was so hot in the classroom due to all the burners that were lit. The next thing I knew, everyone on Kayla's side of the room was screaming. I looked up from my project and saw that Kayla looked like a huge Q-tip on fire! Her whole head of hair was on fire, and there was no saving any of it. The wind from outside was not helping any either. Someone finally got a bucket of water and stuck her whole head down in it. She lost all of her eyebrows and eyelashes. This country girl had never seen anything like that; human destruction in a matter of minutes, and the smell was disgusting.

I can remember when I heard my first car alarm in the city. I asked what the noise was; everyone in Biology class asked me if I had never heard that before? Nope, was it a fire alarm? No, it means someone is breaking into a car in our parking lot out front. I then asked if everyone should not check their vehicles. They told me it would do no good because everything in the car would be gone, and the crooks too by the time they got there. It made no sense to me; why in the world would you have a car alarm on your car then if you were not going to use the darned thing?

I can tell you this, so many things have given me so much joy, but for sure, one of the best gifts ever given to me has been the three grandsons given to me by my daughter and her husband. Those three boys have make me laugh so much and see the world more simply through their eyes.

Skipper can see a frog, and pure magic has happened. His GGma Lene asked him one day if he wanted to take a frog home to Momma. He quickly nodded, yes. She put the frog in a Mallmart bag of all things. The bag had a tiny hole in the bottom, a very tiny hole and a slit on the side, we were sure he could not get out, and Mom tied the top shut. Before he could get settled in his car seat, that darned toad had gotten out of that bag and was in the car seat with Skipper. Skipper was trying to climb on GGG Aunt's head, and Skipper was screaming his head off.

No way he was sitting in that car seat. I got the frog and held it. I told him I would put the frog down on the ground. He sat back in his car seat, and he looked at the toad very warily. He kept watching me, then the toad. I said, say bye to the toad. He waved goodbye to the toad. Great Great Great Aunt buckled him in the car seat, and they took off to go home. I think there will be no further fascination with the toads.

Different than his two older brothers. They would take flashlights and catch over thirty toads in one night and put them in a coffee can and poke breathing holes in the top and get so excited about their night's catch! Then the next morning, I would sneak outside and turn them all loose.

When Gabby was in the hospital with Bishop, Bob, their dad walked into their kitchen at home and found Bobby drinking Spic and Span water from the bucket of dirty water Gabby had been using to mop the floor when she went into labor. Bob sucked in his breath when he saw the sight. The next word out of his mouth was, 'Oh shit.' Bobby was two years old at the time, and the next word out of his mouth at the time was, 'shit.' He had learned his first dirty word — time to call poison control.

Those two boys were a source to reckon with as you never knew what they were going to get in to next. Like the night that Bob and Gabby were in the family room and the boys were all of a sudden 'too quiet.' When Gabby and Bob checked on them, they had cleverly built a scaffold, so they could get up above the washer and dryer and onto the shelf above the two appliances to get the lemon Pledge and spray each other down. They were like greased pigs when Bob and Gabby found them.

They had to call the poison control hotline to find out what to do. It could be absorbed by the liver so quickly. Gabby and Bob could not use warm water, so it had to be cold as the warm or almost hot water would drive it into the skin that much more. Pledge is not so easy to clean off with cold water because it is so oily, so it took a good while to get the two greasy little pigs cleaned up. They were about two and four years old at that time and into everything.

When Bishop was about two or three, he had carried something into the kitchen to show Gabby, and he told her, "Mommy, look what I have." She turned from the sink, and between two fingers, he held the leg of a brown recluse. Gabby being struck with a Mother's pure fear in her heart! She and Bob looked Bishop all over for a bite. They called Poison Control AGAIN. By this time, Poison Control was on speed dial. It had to be; they were calling them all the time. I asked them if you call real often, will they turn you into child services?

Bishop loved Batman; there was nothing you could say about Batman that was negative that he would have ever believed. He wanted everything that had Batman on it. So, one morning before Christmas, the Elf on the Shelf was sitting on top of the living room curtain rod up next to the ceiling holding Bishop's tiny Batman figurine. Bishop was ANGRY. Even at his little age, he had a face when he was angry that there was not a doubt in your mind how he felt. Gabby told him it would be okay. The elf would let Batman go by tomorrow, probably. Everyone went about getting ready for the day. The next thing they knew, Bobby was screaming that Bishop had RUNT Christmas! Bishop had touched the Elf! Clutched in Bishop's hand securely was the Batman figure that Elf on the Shelf had been holding. They all looked on top of the curtain rod, and there sat the Elf where he been all along; he had not moved a bit, but his hostage, Batman, was missing.

They could not figure out how Bishop had climbed up there to get Batman so quickly and retrieve him, but he had! Bobby by then was crying and sobbing and had melted into the floor just like the witch in the famous movie. He knew for sure Christmas was over and never coming again, thanks to Bishop the Evil! I am here to report; however, Christmas did come to their home that year, and Elf on the Shelf did not touch any more of Bishop's Batman toys.

Bishop could climb a slick 10-foot wall. If I did not know any better, I would think he was spiderman himself. That boy could climb anything when he was three years old and not blink an eye. It scared me because he had no fear of climbing anything, but how did he climb the slick surfaces?

When Bishop was about ten years old, they made their annual family pilgrimage to the dentist. Both boys examined, Bobby had been given a clean bill of health. He was the son who NEVER brushed his teeth. But Bishop, well, ten cavities. Bishop brushed his teeth faithfully every day and sometimes twice a day. He was beside himself. He had **ten cavities!** That sounded really serious and maybe even hospital admission and needlesticks. Finally, when he calmed a bit, he said, "What's a cavity?" It wound up they were all in his baby teeth, thank goodness, and he escaped the repair of teeth for now.

A stray kitten appeared at their house one year near Christmas time; it was like a long-haired Siamese, but for sure, no purebred. He was beautiful. When he got loose in the house, the first thing he did was run straight up their nine-foot Christmas Tree from where Daddy Bob had to pull him from among the limbs. They all got attached to the kitten, and since he had shown up at Christmas time, the boys at ages two and four and not being able to pronounce all their letters correctly named him 'Fingle Bells.'

Bob got to be the lucky one for neuter duty, took him to the vet after Christmas to have him neutered, and when they asked Bob what the cat's name was, he replied in a kind of quiet voice to the vet's wife, "Fingle Bells." She laughed out loud and said, "He is not going to be Jingling his Bells for long now, is he?" The entire waiting room thought this was extremely funny.

After several years of living in the house, 'Fingle Bells' started doing something very naughty, and it was the fact that he began peeing on some stuff in the house. That was not a good idea Fingle. Very poor planning on his part with Gabby as his owner and resident housekeeper.

Fingle Bells found himself tossed outside and with him went his feed, water bowls, and even out went his litter pan. Happy Days and times were over. He was now an outside cat! He was now an outie for who knew how long.

Now it is this writer's opinion; maybe you should have him checked for a kidney or bladder stone to make sure he was not trying to tell you he had a urinary tract issue of sorts. Whatever you do, never go to Gabby's house and pee on her mop or her stacked laundry. You might wind up outside with a dish of cat food and if you are lucky a litter pan.

One evening, Bishop was looking out one of the family room windows, and the little guy saw Fingle Bells get run over in the street. He told his Dad that Fingle Bells had got runneded over. Bob ran into the street and scooped Fingle Bells up and brought him back into the house; Fingle Bells was barely clinging to life. He was dying slowly in Bob's arms.

Gabby was getting home from work, but Fingle Bells had held on until she got there to say goodbye to him. They all petted him and said their goodbyes, and he took his last breath before crossing over the rainbow bridge to his permanent place in heaven to wait on his earth family till they got there.

When Skipper came along and just turned three years old, and the whole family was playing a game where you put pieces of boards together and then pull the pieces out a piece at a time without the entire tower collapsing. The game was almost a tie until Bishop, who was on Bob's team, pulled one of the boards, and the walls all came tumbling down, and Bob said, "Shit." Skipper immediately responded with "Shit." How is it you try to teach them other words, and this is the words they learn the quickest?

Skipper proceeded to put all the boards up and was trying to play the game when the walls collapsed, and he immediately said, "SHIT!" He used the word at the proper time and with the right emphasis. Gabby told him that it was not a nice word to use. Skipper looked at her and said, "Sowy."

We had an Aunt and Uncle in the big city that we were very close to, and my aunt was always trying to fix something. My uncle, bless his heart, was no handyman and never pretended to be a handyman. He was my dad's cousin, and they had grown up together. My aunt and my mother were sisters. Almost twins if you saw them. The sisters were born exactly one year, one month, and one day apart, and they married cousins. I loved my aunt and uncle like a second set of parents. My Aunt always made time for me when they came to the country to visit. My parents were so busy trying to make a living on the farm that there was no idle time for them to do anything but work.

When I became an adult and being especially fond of my aunt and uncle, I called them almost every day, sometimes two or three times a day if they weren't feeling good to check on them. After their only child died, I called them even more. On one particular day, I asked my aunt what they had been up to, and she told me something that scares the wits out of me to this day when I realized what had happened to the two of them. I am sure God was watching over them.

My Aunt said that their sewer line had backed up again, and she thought she might know a way to get it unclogged. The product is no longer made (I am very happy about this fact.) and I am sure I understand why it is not. It is a can of something that is highly pressurized (**DANGER #1**), and it contains some chemical in it that warns you that it is highly flammable (**DANGER#2**). My experimental "fix-it" aunt had in her possession a can of this pressurized, flammable something that she thought would unclog HER SEWER! But the product had been made for kitchen sinks. My poor, poor uncle is all I can say; he just followed her to the basement quietly.

I want to add that I hate their basement steps. They are open, and they are steep, and people over the age of 70 or 80 should never go down that terrible precipice of a mountain. No wait, no one over the age of 30 should go down those steps. They scared me to death!

But, here, the two of them go, in the middle of their 70's tottering, dottering down the scary steps with the pressurized, flammable torpedo in my aunt's precious little hand. Let me remind you here that my aunt was NOT a chemist or any kind of education in hazardous chemicals. My uncle, following, believing in her every step of the way. My poor little uncle, who was so educated in journalism, what had happened to him when he said, "I do?"

My aunt had read on the can that you are to pump the can twice over your kitchen drain to unclog it, and since she was trying to unclog the entire sewer system of the City they lived in then she would pump it up five or six times. And, she did just that. My uncle, never a man to tell an untruth a day in his life, said to me, "It was just like in the movies. The flames danced all around us in the entire basement in a large circle in all colors, and they stayed suspended in the air for quite some time. When the fire had subsided, and they both came back to their selves, Aunt looked up from her bent over position and said, 'Do I have any eyelashes? Did it get my hair?' He assured her that it did not get her hair or her eyelashes, but he did not know how the hair was still on her head." He then said she looked at him and very solemnly stated, "I will never complain again about the price of homeowner's insurance." I can tell you that to this day, I know she has not.

My aunt told me the whole time the flames were dancing in rings around them covering the entire basement, and their basement is quite large; my uncle was standing there perfectly calm with his hands in his pockets like he was visiting and talking to someone as if there was no inferno around them in the basement.

After it was over and my uncle had thought about it, he said he realized it was pretty scary. I said to them, "Did you ever think with all that methane gas in the sewer system you could have blown up your house or maybe even the entire city?" Neither of them had even given it a thought that they could have blown up their entire house. All that would have found were two charred little skeletons in the basement with one holding an aerosol can in her hand bent over the sewer drain. Goes to prove, life can suck you away in a matter of seconds.

Having the two of them in my life has brought me so many laughs that I cannot begin to remember all of them. My aunt is obsessive-compulsive to the extreme unless she takes her medication as prescribed. When it comes to cleaning, dressing, baking, sewing, and about every area of her life, everything has to be done in a certain order. But cleaning is by far the worse. One day my uncle said to me, "If there were such a thing as reincarnation, I would be afraid I would come back as a piece of Formica, and she would be the one who cleaned me all the time."

He also had the wise theory that life was way too short to

spend in a fabric or craft store and that no one should be in such establishment for more than ten minutes before 'cashing out' as my daughter told him when she was five.

I know that when I tell some of these stories, you are going to say, "I find that hard to believe." I promise you, they are all true, or may God strike me with lightning, and how in the world could I make this stuff up? It is too crazy!

One summer, we decided we would all go to a big theme park as a big family. It sounded like a lot of fun. Gabby was about two or two and a half. The day started as a lot of fun. As the day heated up, so did people's tempers flare. My Uncle, myself, and Gabby were standing in a large opening waiting for the rest of our group to gather. Remember, this was before cell phones even! Gee, how did we exist? While standing there, a very large woman and several of her family members got into a ferocious fight. I mean a serious one, more serious than I had ever been exposed to in my naïve life. There were small children present, and there were some really bad words being used that little ones should not be hearing.

I thought, this woman is really angry about something, and I think she is in the mood to hit about anyone who would cross her path! I think she could take me down in one smack. About that time, my Uncle looked at me and said as loud as he could, "That is what I like about theme parks. Families come together where they can have fun and fellowship, and there is no fighting or screaming and cursing around others in the Park."

The lady looked up as she was standing behind my Uncle. I just knew she was going to split his head open. I was ready to get the heck out of there but I had to make sure she did not make a dive for my Uncle. Holy Moly! What was I going to do? I knew I was a goner if she came after him. About that time, several of the adult men in our group showed up, and I was never so glad to see them in all my life. Uncle never got one feather ruffled, and I wanted to have stress diarrhea all over the park. This girl was sure it was all going down right then and there — news at eleven.

One summer, we decided we were all going to get healthy and start riding bikes on the farm. We were going to ride about 3 – 6 miles a day, so we all got mountain bikes. There were five of us out riding. We didn't stay together, but we all rode at the same time and at different paces. That year was good for the local chain store for selling mountain bikes and not bad for cassette players, portable CD players, and headphone business either.

One particular summer evening, we had all finished riding, and Mom and Dad were the very last to come in from biking their miles. I could not imagine what had made them so late coming in as they had started a little later than the rest of us, but not that much. When they got back, my Dad was dripping with blood from his face, his arms, his back, and his chest. He was covered in blood. He looked like a polecat had scratched him up but good. We did have a lot of bobcats and a few mountain lions in the area, but Mom was untouched.

Mother said there were man-eating blackberry vines along their biking path that reached out and grabbed Dad and just kept pulling him into the vines. Said they were huge vines with the biggest thorns you have ever seen! They kept tearing at his skin, and they had no way to cut the vines, and they had to unwrap him from each vine, and as they did, another vine would grab him from another direction. He looked terrible with all the scratches and the bleeding. He did not ride bikes for a long time.

One summer, Mom, Dad, myself, Gabby, Bob, Bobby, and Bishop rented a cottage at the beach in Destin, Florida. It was a three-story, and we decided to take Jenny, Mom and Dad's Jack Russell, their German Shepherd Pup Nicki, and Gabby and Bob's Wermeriner Cocoa. The ride down was not bad. We had sedated them all pretty good on the way down with Benedryl, and they all slept most of the way. I wish they had given me Benedryl.

When we got to Destin, we all got into the town-house, and we loved the place. The dogs were precious, or kind of, sort of, I guess. One of them and my gut tells me it was Nicki because she was a puppy chewed my power cord to my computer in two parts. NOT GOOD. The boys and I were going to play some fun 'seek and search' games, and here we were without a power cord. So, I went to a radio shack and bought a power cord pack that would fit any computer.

The next evening we made a stupid decision to go to the beach with all our dogs on leashes. We were a happy family walking our dogs on the beach. What a picture we made. Yeah, right! What idiots we were, thinking this would last! Cocoa, the Wermeiriner, loved the water, but of course, she was a Wermeiriner and loved the water! Then Cocoa DRANK the water in the ocean. A HUGE no-no for dogs at the beach; we had no idea that it would cause real problems.

All of a sudden, Cocoa began having explosive diarrhea on the beach! It shot out of her at least 3 to 4 feet everywhere; it seemed like it was a big fountain and shooting all over the sand with beachgoers everywhere! Bob, my son-in-law, grabbed her leash and said, "Cocoa, home!" It was too late. Diarrhea was washing into the sea, and swimmers were all running to get out of the water where we were standing.

All of a sudden, our entire family was an Ebola Contagion Group standing alone on the shores of Destin, Florida. We all high tailed it back to our beach house, closed our curtains, locked our doors, and stayed there, and the dogs did not go back to the beach. We took them for walks, but NOT back to the beach. I promise you this happened. This is where the country met the city, and the country should have stayed back at their beach house with their dogs.

I remember the day Mom and Dad got their little Jack Russell dog. She was just a puppy. They were so proud of her. Mom said to me, "Guess what her name is." I said, "I have no idea. What is it?" She said, "Go ahead and guess." I said, "Mom, I can't imagine. You tell me." She said, "Her name is Nicki." It was hard holding back the smile. A Jack Russell Dog named Nicki.

The first thing that happened to the little thing was she ran into my English Springer Spaniel, Petunia, who was getting old and hateful and was annoyed with a new pup. The spaniel picked up little Nicki and shook her like a rag! For NO reason. It almost knocked her eye out of her little tiny head. The poor little thing. Right off the bat to the vet. She lost most of the vision in that eye, thanks to a cranky old dog. I felt terrible about it.

Dogs and cats are a lot like humans. When they get old, they get dementia; they get tired, they hurt, they don't want to be around those young ones that remind them of their lost youth. Slap them out of your way! Or, in this case, pick them up in your mouth and shake the fire out of them!

Haven't you seen old folks in the nursing home like that? On a visit to my uncle, I walked past one elderly ladies' room, and she started chasing me down the hall, screaming. I ran to the nurse's station as fast as I could. I asked them why she was chasing me. They told me I was short, like the woman her husband ran off with. Every time I went back, I was careful at what angle I went when I walked by her room.

By all standards, everyone in the family said that Nicki was very spoiled. The only dog baby on the dead-end road. Mom and Dad's baby. She was always in someone's lap. Dad even built her a special place to ride on his tractor so she could sit or stand on it and not fall off when she rode the tractor with him. When the tractor started up, she thought he could not go forward unless she was in her seat! She was a hot, cute mess.

Her time in Destin was not without drama, however. Let me tell you! She was not Gabby's favorite pet of her grandparents. She and her new husband 'house sat' for Grandma and Grandpa while we were all out of state at a large teaching hospital for reasons of Dad's leukemia. Nicki was still a new puppy and was being housebroken.

She made sure to give Gabby plenty of practice in cleaning up after her. Gabby said that every time Nicki needed to go potty, she would get in front of Gabby and go. I heard about this every time I called home to check on how things were going. She and Gabby never got along after that week. For all the years that Nicki lived, Gabby and Nicki were not best friends.

So, while in Destin one day, Mom, Dad, and I went out shopping while Gabby, Bob, and the boys went out on the beach. When they got back to the beach house, they could not believe it! Nicki darted through their legs and ran away! Bob and Gabby could not believe what had just happened. They put the boys inside and told them to watch TV, not to move, and they would

be right back. Gabby said she could NOT tell her Grandpa
that they had lost his most beloved pet at the beach! They
ran everywhere. Bob would run one street and Gabby another
calling Nicki's name as they went. They would see her at the end
of one alleyway and then at the other end of a street. Always far
away. They kept running. What were they going to do? They
were coming back to the beach house when Bob happened to see
Nicki approaching a group of older women, and he was able to
sneak up on Nicki and grab her.

She got her butt brought back to the beach house, and Gabby,
sweet, demure, little Gabby I am sure did not have kind words
to say to Nicki who had escaped merely to look for her beloved
Master, Grandpa. Gabby and Bob had both sweated so much
from running and were so exhausted that every time anyone
opened the main entrance door for the rest of the vacation, they
would holler, "Where is Nicki?" An experience like that will do
something to you that will last you the rest of your life. I think
they developed Doggie PTSD from that vacation as they both
have been odd about small dogs ever since that vacation and
only purchase large dogs.

I can remember when it was Bishop's first day of Preschool,
so that meant it was Bobby's first day of second grade. They
both had their packbacks on, the first day of school pictures had
been taken by no other but a proud Momma.

Their Daddy, a very tall man was telling them with most of it
directed to Bishop that they had to pay attention to the teacher,
they could not talk; they would have to wait until snack time
to eat; they would have to raise their hand and wait till their
teacher called their name before they could speak. The boys
would need to be kind to the other kids, and be sure to keep
up with each other and get on the same bus if mom or dad did

not get there to pick them up. Bishop, with his big brown eyes, looked up at Bob while he was letting his backpack slide off his shoulders and said, "I don't think I can do all of this."

During that school year, Gabby was unpacking Bishop's backpack to see if there were any notes from the teacher or if he had any homework in it. When she unzipped it, she found an entire BIG box of cereal inside. Gabby asked Bishop why he had taken a whole box of cereal to school. He calmly replied, "Mom, they don't feed you at that school, and I get so hungry. I had to take something to eat."

As Bobby and Bishop grew up, we as grandparents could not let them grow up, and they still wanted a bottle after their mother had "weaned" them at home. When they spent the night at my house or Ma Lene's and Pa Walter's, they still got a bottle. We would hide them when their mom and dad were around. After all, what happens at Grandma's and Grandpas' stays and Grandmas' and Grandpas.'

One night Bobby was spending the night with me, his Noni. Bobby was so cute standing there at the front window waving goodbye to his Mom and Dad; there, he stood all dressed in his little blue jean shorts and a T-shirt looking so precious. After their car lights disappeared down the road, he turned to me and said, "I think this would be a good time for a bottle." I agreed and went promptly and made him a bottle of chocolate milk, and he was one happy little boy.

The summer when Bobby was four and Bishop was two, their little family and my Mom, Dad, and I all went on vacation to the Mountains with our final destination being to wind up in a City close by so that the boys could spend the night on a choo-choo train. It was to celebrate Bobby having been potty trained, but it had taken a long time to get around to having the chance to make the trip. I had also promised him we would all ride a train as well.

We hid bottles for fresh milk and took cocoa for their bottles at night then too. It was tough hiding the bottles all the time. The boys would get the bottles in their mouths, and Gabby would pop her head into the room, and we would have to hide them under the covers. We would be giggling, and they would think it was so funny, and when she would leave, we would laugh some more.

That was such a precious time, and I shall never forget it. The boys were little then, and they were so much fun to be with, and you could get them to do all kinds of stuff with you. They were at the age that they made you feel young again too.

One summer, when we went to the Mountains, we stayed in a log cabin up in the mountains. The cabin was gorgeous, and the area was beautiful. We had wildlife right in the yard all the time. We would sleep in and then go about what we were going to do during the day or the night. One evening we ALL went to the House of what I call Plum Crazy because I can't remember the name of this place, and one of the first things you had to do was walk through a tunnel that was swirling around you as you walked across a bridge.

We all made it to the other side and realized we had lost GMa. Bob Lee said he would go back in and find her. Bob was to be her hero. Back into the moving tunnel, he went. When he got to GMa, he found her clinging to life itself as the swirling tunnel had her so dizzy that she could not go any farther than where she had made it, where Bob found her, a few feet inside the beginning of the tunnel. Bob saved the evening.

There is truly not a lot of nightlife on this dead-end road, but we have so much fun with what we did do at night. I loved to frog gig, and so did Gabby when she got older. I did not like the beavers that would come along and try to slap their tails on the water and get you to leave. I was always worried they were going to flip the canoe over as they were big beavers. Dad always had things under control, but the beavers were so quiet when they topped the water and slapped their tails so much so that it still scared you.

We also had stump burnings, and with every stump burning, we had hot dog roastings and even toasted some marshmallows. Every time we had a stump to burn, we took the opportunity to make a party out of it. That is entertainment for real country folks. It sounds boring to those in the city, but I can promise you it is not. It is some of the most relaxing wood-burning, story telling time you will ever partake of in your life.

One summer, when Brylee was about four years old, I was getting ready to bathe him in the whirlpool tub and filled it with bubbles. He could hardly wait. Talk about excited! I went into the bathroom to help him, and he told me I had to leave. I left the bathroom as he said, and in a few minutes, he called me back in, and there he stood stark naked, spread all four like for a cop to search him. I asked him why he had me leave the room, and he told me so he could take off his clothes. I had to go back into the living room so I could laugh. He said, "Dranma, can you put me in the tub?" I went back in and placed him in the tall tub, and he had bubbles as long as he wanted to play. Every grandchild has loved that tub EXCEPT, my youngest, and he hates it with a passion. Screams his head off, just looking at it.

Birthdays were always a big deal for the grandkids in our family, and we made sure that every birthday was celebrated because that person had been with us one more year, and we prayed they would be healthy, and God would grant them to be with us another. The particular birthday of one red-headed boy requested that he wanted a John Deere birthday party and cake. John Deere, it was because he loved anything, John Deere. The top of his cake was painted with a John Deere tractor on top. It was a sheet cake. Bishop was so small at the time he was puttering around on the floor while everyone was getting ready for the party. When Mom, Dad, and birthday boy came back into the dining area to pick up the cake and leave, Bishop was sitting on the snack bar and no one could figure out how he got there. It was impossible at his age. He had been eating. He took his fingers and ran them down the entire center of the John Deere cake, messing up the image at the zero hour.

About the 7th of November, my Chocolate Lab, Hershey, came to the side of my bed, trying to awaken me. It was tough to wake up because of the fatigue from my disease, but Hershey did not give up. She started barking, and when that did not work, she began lunging at my bed and pushed the mattress partially off the box springs. I was sure that there had to be something wrong for her to have tried to push my mattress off the box springs and barking so much.

I got out of the bed to follow her into the dining room and stepped into water, a lot of water, and on into the kitchen to hear water gushing from somewhere around the dishwasher. I walked down my basement stairs and water was standing in my family room in the basement, and my fish in the 70-gallon aquarium was swimming for all they were worth to try and stay in the aquarium as it had become a vast waterfall from water running from upstairs down into the basement straight into the aquarium.

My beautiful Hershey and what she had done for me. Had it not been for her waking me up how many more hours would this have gone on before I would have awakened and even recognized anything like this had happened.

I lost this beautiful creature a couple of years later to lung cancer. That dog will be forever etched in my mind as she knew me better than I knew myself. I was so lucky to have had her for my friend. I am sure she will be waiting for me at Heaven's gates. The bond we had was very special.

One spring morning in 1992, Dad brought me a slick little animal he was carrying in his shirt pocket. At first, I was not sure what it was until I got a good look at it. I recognized it was a tiny baby opossum. He said its mother had gotten run over on the blacktop near our home, and it was the only one of the babies that had survived. He went on to say that it was sitting up on the momma possum's side and looking around as if to convey, "what do I do now?"

A possum queen was born that day, and that would be me. If you want my true title, I am the "Possum Queen of Our County." I have a strong competitor for that title, so she must be watched carefully so that the crown is not taken from my head, right, TC? I fell in love with that baby possum. She became a member of our family right away. She loved being held, loved to be rocked, she never considered herself to be a possum. She thought she was one of us.

I trained her to a litter pan right off the bat, and it took little effort. She caught on right away. When it got supper time, she would come to the dining table and hold her hand out for her bologna sandwich (she would only eat one brand of lunch meat - KC Bologna), and she would sit on her hind legs and eat her sandwich with her two little hands like a person right there by the table in the floor with the rest of the family.

She was so clean and tidy in taking care of her hygiene. Never let anyone tell you a possum is not a clean animal as they are one of the cleanest you will ever find. She bathed regularly all day long, and she loved getting baths with perfumed soaps. When I would wash her pouch, she always acted as it tickled her because she would scrunch up, and it looked like she was grinning.

I would dress her up in doll clothes and take her to the local elementary school for show and tell on request. She was always a hit with the kids. But Petunia had one thing on her mind all the time, and that was eating. She could not stop eating. She loved lots of food, I tell you. Her preference was KC bologna, though, and you better not try OM or any other big name brand. She liked strawberry jam on bread, but not toast. She did not like generic brands of strawberry jam; she wanted the real thing. She loved marshmallows like they were going out of style and ate them as there would never be any more.

But the poor girl, she got to weighing over 30 pounds! That is very oversized for a possum.

Gabby's first year in college, during the summer, she only had to take pharmacology, so she had a little extra time on her hands, and she spent a lot of it with our pastor's wife. They lived just across the field from us; out in the country, you don't have blocks or down by the stoplight or over on the next street. You have this county road, this blacktop, or by this field or across the field — a whole new ball game when you step into the country. I promise on my Bibles.

The preacher's wife called Gabby one morning and told her there was a mother dog at her house, a German Shepherd that had come to them and just started having puppies. Puppies! Gabby said, "Did you say puppies?" Her face lit up, she grabbed her car keys, and off to the preacher's house, she went.

The German Shepherd who was later named Ruthie because she reminded me so much of one of my great aunt's. So humble and so kind. Ruthie had 13 puppies. She just kept having one baby after another! It was like she was never going to stop. Pastor's wife said, "What are we going to do with all these puppies, Gabby? You know my husband is going to kill me?" Gabby assured her he would not kill her and that she, Gabby, would help with finding homes for all of them. Yep, sure she would like it to stop snowing or raining. I knew exactly what would happen. Those dogs were going to live at our house forever. It would be like every other stray that crossed our driveway entrance.

All was going well with mother and babies until one morning early before we were leaving for work when the pastor's wife called and told Gabby that there were four puppies dead. They were with the mother and dead — no obvious reason. The pastor's wife and Gabby sprang into action. Ruthie and the remaining puppies were rushed to the veterinarian to find out what was going on.

Much to the Pastor's wife and Gabby's dismay, Ruthie was diagnosed with mastitis, an infection of the mammary glands, and that was killing the puppies. Gabby and the pastor's wife now had nine baby puppies that had to be bottle-fed around the clock. The vet bill was already starting to add up. Gabby held out her hand toward us for a check. The bill was too big for cash.

Special milk powder had to be purchased, and as the puppies grew, we went through more milk powder that had to be mixed fresh each feeding. Gabby took five, and the preacher's wife took four to raise. Ruthie, somewhere along the way, came to live at our house too. A decision I have never regretted. She was the most amazing dog I had ever been around. She was so very smart and looked at me like she understood every word I was saying.

Gabby was busy all the time; up all hours of the night feeding puppies, washing laundry for their bedding, going to college, rushing back home the twenty-six miles and feeding puppies, and washing more bedding. They were her babies that summer. Of course, she decided to name her puppies after the knights of the round table since she had been reading a book on the subject.

Then, ALL the puppies got dysentery. Yes, that is what I said dysentery. In simple terms, they all had diarrhea at the same time and it smelled bad, and it was NASTY! Gabby loaded all nine puppies in a wicker bassinet and back to the veterinarian they went. They had some bacterial infection, and of course, now they were all on liquid medication for several days. That meant more laundry since they were soiling their bedding more frequently.

I have to admit; the puppies were gorgeous. The puppies were big balls of fur and so beautiful. They were all sure that Gabby was their momma, and when she took them outside to play, they followed her everywhere.

As they grew, the itching began, in all nine puppies. The odd part of it was that they did not live near each other. Some lived here, and some lived across the field. But, they all got mange at the same time. The next thing we knew, we hosted a puppy baptizing in our backyard for all nine puppies. What an evening that was, and the medicated water smelled so nasty.

Preacher's wife and Gabby found homes for almost all of them except Ruthie.

Ruthie had some sort of congenital heart problem that when she would walk across the backyard, she would fall over and pass out. She would lay there for a minute and get back up as if nothing had happened. The veterinarian was never for sure what the heart problem was but felt sure she had had it all her life.

One day while Gabby's step-dad was working on our bass boat getting it ready for the weekend, he had to pull it forward to work on the tires. He had no idea that Ruthie was anywhere around. When he pulled forward, he ran over Ruthie's head. He felt terrible and wanted to get her to the vet immediately. He knew that Ruthie and I had a "connection." He finally called me at work and asked me if I could leave work early as she would not get in the car for him. He could not get her to do anything.

I drove as fast as I legally could to get home to my Ruthie girl, wondering what kind of damage a heavy fiberglass boat had done to her head. My imagination went wild. When I got home to her, I opened the back door of the car, and she hopped right into the back seat. Bless her heart; she was such an obedient dog. I loved her so much.

We got to our vet, and she walked right in with me. I felt tears sting my eyes as she obeyed my every command. She had to be in terrible pain, but yet, she was doing everything that I had asked her to do.

Our vet checked her over and x-rayed her, and the boat had broken her one jaw. I was ecstatically happy and shocked that her skull was not damaged. We had to leave her, and she had to go into surgery for her jaw to be wired shut, and we could pick her up the next day.

So, the next morning, we picked her up, and she was glad

to see us, we were required to feed her for the next six weeks by hand soft canned dog food because her jaw had to be wired shut until it healed. Bless her heart; that beautiful heart beating inside her chest had to be designed from gold.

But, that was not to be the end of Ruthie's troubles. It was necessary to check Gabby's step Dad's blood every couple of weeks because of blood thinners that he was on, and I had a hard container that I put the used needles in when finished with them. One morning after taking his blood, I thoughtlessly laid the used needle on the window sill in the kitchen, thinking I would throw it away in a bit and never thought of it again.

The housekeeper that came every other week came and left. I never thought of anything AGAIN about that stinkin needle!

On another evening coming home from work, Ruthie met me, clawing at her mouth and acting like she had something stuck between her teeth. I looked inside her mouth and could not see anything. I could not get her to eat her favorite food. Something was wrong.

Again, I asked her to get in the back seat of the car, and she obliged as my Ruthie would. Again, we made the trip to the vet fifteen miles away. Our vet looked inside and could not see a thing and was about to give up and say he was going to put her to sleep and do a scope on her when he caught a glimpse of something. Sure enough, she had swallowed something, and it was a used needle that we used to draw blood from a vein.

It had been thrown in the trash, gotten put into the burn bin, and something in the burn bin smelled good to Ruthie, and she decided to get a taste of it, and the needle was in the middle of whatever she tasted.

The needle in the throat called for endoscopic surgery and a night in the vet hospital, and again we were to pick her up in the morning, as good as new.

We worked in high-stress jobs Monday through Friday, and that is why we look forward to vacation so we can go live somewhere else and have different stress for a few days, and then we are so glad to be back home. I remember those days so well. I loved vacation time.

Now, just thinking about packing up for a vacation makes me tired. Thinking about driving or standing in line at the airport makes me tired. If I could blink myself there and "be" there, it would be ok. But, as it is, the whole thing makes me tired.

Gabby and Bob had only been married for about seven months, and we asked them to go on vacation with us, and they did not have to pay for anything but their gas to the Island and back home.

Bob did not get off work until late that afternoon, and they had decided to drive after he got off work. They arrived at about 2:00 in the morning and were both tired. I was so glad to see them and know they were with us and safe.

They came with a surprise to the beach house that year. Before they left their home, they had found a squirrel that had fallen from a tree in front of their apartment and broke its front leg. They had rescued the squirrel and brought it along with them on vacation in a cage.

The little squirrel was an angry little squirrel, might I add. It was a female, and after much debate, we decided to name her, after my mother. When you got close to her cage, she would jump at the side of the cage and make a loud hissing sound.

The squirrel, loved peanut butter, so every morning, Gabby would get up and feed my mother's name sake a big spoon full of peanut butter. However, one morning, for some reason, the sneaky little squirrel got out of the cage and was running all through the beach house. It was a pretty big beach house. It had three large bedrooms, three baths, a very large kitchen, and dining area and a large living room so the squirrel could outrun you very easy.

The squirrel, had a lot of places to run. All I am going to say is that with a broken leg, she may not be able to climb, but by golly, she sure could run fast! Nobody could catch her until Bob finally did, and he had on metal gloves made for handling wildlife, and that stinkin' squirrel still bit through that glove! Then Bob worried the rest of the vacation that he might have contracted rabies, BUT he didn't.

That was the same year that Grandma decided to wear her clogs with wooden soles inside the beach house, and the beach house had wood floors. She got up before anyone else in the mornings, and it sounded like someone hammering nails into the floor every morning, and it woke up everyone. Bob decided this would not happen again, it was vacation, and he wanted to sleep in, and so did everyone else.

The clogs with the wooden soles disappeared. NO ONE knew what had happened to them. No one could find them. It was a mystery. But, they did show up the morning we were packing to come home — such a mystery.

It was this vacation that we put jigsaw puzzles together during the hottest parts of the day and the year that my Aunt went with us on vacation. We worked so hard on one of the puzzles. We would even work late at night on any of the puzzles, and if we got one done, we would get another one out and put it together. One particular puzzle we worked on, Dad was lying on the couch, and for some reason, just happened to see Bob take a puzzle piece and hide it from everyone. Dad never said anything to anyone, but quiet when we were about to get done with the puzzle, he went and picked up the puzzle piece that Bob had hidden and placed it back on the table where we were working on the puzzle itself without anyone noticing what he had done.

When we put the last piece in, Bob was so shocked he couldn't believe it! All of us except Dad were unaware of what Bob had done, so we could not figure out why he was so shocked. He ran to where he had hidden the puzzle piece, and it was gone. No one was saying anything, and Dad was lying on the couch, still reading his book. Bob still not figuring out how that puzzle piece got back on the table.

At the end of the week, Dad finally broke his silence, and the mystery of the puzzle piece was revealed. It gave everyone a real laugh because Bob was always pulling a trick on someone.

We went out into the bay and fished that summer in Dad's bay boat. That was ridiculous fun. I will never forget the good times we had on the boat for as long as I live, but that summer with Aunt and Bob added so much more fun. When Aunt went out on the boat, she was dog sick. She could even see the shoreline and still got dog sick. Wet wash rags on her forehead did not help either. She was plain seasick.

When we went out night fishing, she made sure she took medicine so she would not be seasick. She was as green as a head of cabbage if she did not take the meds.

While we were out night fishing, Bob caught a pink snake, so he hooked the snake right and dangled it in Aunt's face. I honestly thought she was going to leave the boat and jump into the water in the middle of the night, not knowing what fish was out there to eat her. Aunt, at age 79 was not a very good swimmer especially out in the deeper part of the ocean.

One summer, we were on the beach, and our pastor, his wife, and three-year-old daughter were with us. Dad and mom had already gone to bed, and Dad had already taken his medications for the night which included a sleeping pill. This particular night Dad had decided to leave the boat anchored out behind the beach house instead of loading it out at the marina.

Someone noticed that the boat had come in with the surf and was almost beached. We would have to get it back out in the ocean before the inboard motor got full of sand. So, some of us were in the water trying to get it pushed back out in the ocean.

Mom went back to the beach house and got Dad up, never should this have been done, there were others of us who knew how to drive the boat and the truck and trailer but here he came stumbling down the tall deck steps from the beach house, and when he got to the water's edge, he stumbled and crawled, fell over into the boat with our pastor, Gabby, and myself. Before we knew what was happening, Dad was starting up the boat. What in the world was he doing?

At this point, I seriously thought he was going to move the boat out further into the bay. It was not and could NOT leave this area. His night time medications made him act like a drunken sailor. Now mind you I had never seen a drunken sailor, but I would bet money this is what a drunken sailor would be like exactly. We had **NO** lights on the boat; we could not see where we were even going. The only light in our possession was the little tiny headlight thingy that our preacher had, and it was like holding a match in the wind.

Dad did not take off slowly. He took off pushing the throttle to top speed headed toward the marina. I was not sure what would happen next. I was not sure what was happening right then. What in the world was he doing? Those of us who were not acting like drunken sailors had no clue. We could not see anything. There was no moon to shine on the water. No lights out near the beach houses. How could we see the rock jetties that ran out from the beach. If we hit one of them, we would all die instantly. None of us had grabbed our life jackets off the deck when we walked down to the boat.

About that time, our pastor took his tiny little flashlight, headlight thingy and shined it toward the beach, and right there was a rock jetty, next to the boat. Dear Lord in heaven! When I say this I say it with every bit of breath in my lungs leaving. I could not take my next breath and felt very faint. We were about to crash, and we had a drugged Captain. The preacher screamed, I screamed, and Gabby was in the bottom of the boat on her knees, praying out loud. Seriously, praying out loud as fast as she could pray in all earnest.

I promise anyone reading this book that the only way we got around all those rock jetties, around the end of the fort, and back up to the marina safely was because God laid His hand on us and was protecting us every step of the way. I know this for sure because there was no other way possible. You would know it was true if you had been there with us. It was the most frightening ride of my entire life, and I have had some scary things happen to me.

I am positive that when we pulled up into the marina that there were three of us, NOT the Captain, that had turned white as a bleached sheet. I felt that all the blood had drained entirely away from my body and that I would not be able to stand on my legs ever again. My legs felt like they had been made of jello. I wanted to get out when I was able to walk and kiss the sand because I was so thankful to be alive.

Gabby had been in college and was 20-21 years old and had decided she would move to a small nearby town in the neighboring state. She got a job at a local hospital while she was going to nursing school to help pay for her apartment and her gas money and so forth.

Her working at the hospital helped her decide her career path. At that time, the little hospital was more like a nursing home. Gabby could not stand anyone throwing up. When she had to clean up vomit, Gabby would vomit with the patient, making a bigger mess than ever to clean up, and the other nurses would tell her to stop, and they would clean up the mess.

She finally gave in and said she was just not cut out for nursing. She could not deal with all the sputum, vomit, and other body fluids that came from others. It made her sick all the time, and she could not eat. She lost so much weight that she could not be a nurse in her mind. So, I had a beautiful daughter who was almost an RN. When she got married, many of the decorations were small glass green frogs to honor the fact she liked frog gigging with her grandpa, and one of them held a sign that said, "Gabby, Almost RN."

When she left home, she took her 'Cimaron' cat and her orange 'Cat.' She left her dog with us. When she would come home in the evenings or on weekends, she would sneak them out of her "no pets allowed" apartment in an overnight bag and bring them home for a visit. One of the nights she got back to her apartment with Cimaron and Cat, Cimaron managed to unzip the overnight case and poke her head out!

Then, one day, on getting back to her apartment to change to go to work at the hospital, she noticed Cimaron was setting up in the window. HUGE give away to the landlord with a no pet policy. Gabby warned Cimaron that she was going to get them kicked out of the apartment. It didn't matter. Cimaron kept sitting up in the window. Finally, Gabby brought Cat and Cimaron back home and said she had to leave them here ONLY until she could move somewhere that accepted pets because Cimaron was going to get her thrown out.

Take it from me, as a parent of a kid moving out of the home, you should NEVER believe a line like that from your child! I can tell you right now; they are **lying** to you without knowing they are lying to you. They have good intentions in those five minutes when they are telling you the lie. After that five minutes has passed, they will never again think of that moment no matter how many times you remind them for the next fifteen years. There was always an excuse, not a good reason, but still an excuse.

Cimaron lived to be 22 years old, at my house no less. She was as blind as she could be, and I was her waitress and nurse. She was deaf in one ear. I noticed something was wrong when she started sleeping on one of my kitchen cabinets of all places and would never get down except at night to use the litter pan so the dogs would not bother her. I had a huge roll around birdcage, so I fixed it up for her with everything a cat should need to be happy living in, and she seemed so satisfied. She lived in that cage for seven years and died October of 2019, fifteen minutes before I was to leave for church. I could not stand thinking she would be here by herself when she passed. I had prayed that God would allow me to be with her when she passed, and he granted my prayer. Cimaron taught me a lot of lessons about life. She taught me:

- About patience. She only liked drinking ice water, always had from a kitten till now. Nothing else would do, and she would ask for ice water about four times a day. She was so patient after she told you she wanted some ice water. She would sit by her water bowl that hung on the side of the cage and patiently wait. She would be delighted when you got there with her ice. It always sounded like she said, 'Thank you.'
- To always be grateful to those who care for you. If she wet the pads in her cage or soiled them the slightest, she let you know. It was a different meow. She was not as

patient when that happened, and I do not blame her in the slightest. I tried to take care of that problem pronto. I would not want that in my bed if I were confined. As soon as you would clean it up, it sounded like she said, "Thank You" again.

- <u>Never assume someone is going to adopt you as their friend</u>. If you did not know her and she did not know your smell, she had no claws, but she could hit you harder with her front paws than a boxer in the ring. She was a tough little thing up until the last five days. She was so thin the previous five years that you could read a newspaper through her.
- <u>She taught me that it did not matter how your hair looked every day</u>. Just go with how it looked and live every day like it was your last. If I tried to comb her hair or cut out the matted hairpieces, she would even hit me with her little fist. She did not want her hair/fur touched!
- <u>No matter how old you are, your taste can change</u>. Until the last couple of months before she passed, all her life, she had only eaten dry cat food. She would never touch canned cat food, milk, or cat treats. But the last two months, she started asking for shredded salmon canned cat food, not pate' but shredded.
- <u>When you leave this world to go live with the Lord, there is no fear</u>. For five nights, she asked to sleep with me so that I would lift her in the bed, and she would get close to me and sleep there all night long. She had never done that before in her 22 years. I knew her time was short. The day before she passed, she went into a semi-coma, so I sat up that night with her in case she should need comforting. The next morning she was not responding to any stimuli, and by 10:15, she took her last breath. I could not cry for her, I had been doing that the last five days. She had been the sweetest and best cat ever, and to have lived for 22 years says a lot. I think about her every

day, and when I get up, I still go in the direction of where her cage sat to see if she needs ice water. No telling how long I will do that.

My cousin had come from the city to go to my work party with me on the weekend. We did not stay late, but when we got home and pulled into my driveway, we were both shocked at what we saw in front of us. My driveway consists of a small chat that has a lot of powder-like substance in it that turns into concrete, so it makes a hard driveway for you.

There in front of us was a possum's head sticking up out of the chat driveway, and the head was turning around and around, eyes open and hissing at us. What in the world was going on? Was someone pulling a crazy joke on us? My cousin, a real city girl, jumped out of the car when I did and went forward to make sure what we were seeing was real. About that time, our big yellow lab (remember the World's Greatest Hunting Dog), came running up and looked things over and then looked at us as if to say, "so what do you girls think about my handy work?" That dog had dug a perfectly round hole like he had used a post hole digger and bore straight down, then shoved that possums butt down in the hole and packed him in there like a sausage in a package. He was packed in that hole like someone had poured concrete around him. My cousin said what in the world are we going to do? He is right in the center of where you drive in to get in your garage. You can't drive over him with the car.

The yellow lab even looked at me as if to say, "Yeah, what are going to do with my possum? It took me a long time to plant that possum!" I grabbed the possum up by the scruff of the neck and started to wiggle him to freedom. Our yellow lab looked terrified. He could not believe I was taking his possum away from him. My cousin said, "You better not do that; it is

going to bite you!" I told her that it would not bite me. I had
not been bitten by a possum yet. I finally freed the possum and
held onto it by the scruff of the neck and held it under its bum.
I started walking to the car and got into the passenger side and
asked cousin to drive the car down the road to the west so we
could set the possum free.

City cousin got behind the wheel, and I held onto the freed
possum by the neck and under it's back, hoping it felt fairly
comfortable. I talked to it softly, and it never acted frightened.
When we got to where we needed to be, I asked my cousin to
please stop the car. She reached out and opened my door, and we
walked over to the road ditch together. There I let the possum
down, and it shook itself off like its hair was messed up, and
then it walked off into the dark. Nothing is ever calm on this
dead-end road. There is at least one crazy show a day.

City, cousin, is the one who brought me the cat Liz Borden
from a home where she was being abused. The owner was
throwing her against the walls of his apartment, and the kitten
was so tiny. No one ever put food in her or her brother's food
bowl or water in the water bowl. Instead, they both slept in
their dishes, and even when Liz came to live with me, she kept
sleeping in a bowl if she could find one. Liz and her brother had
both been abused and starved.

My uncle took her brother, and I agreed to Liz. When Liz got
old enough, I had her declawed and spayed. She was the cutest
little kitten you have ever seen. She had a bobbed tail.

Liz grew and grew after coming to live here. She was turning
into a beautiful cat. For the brother-sister duo, she was staying
pretty small while her brother was getting massive. He was
getting so large he could not clean himself good, so he was being
taken to a groomer to be trimmed and cleaned now and then.

Liz was not without her faults, however. She was honery. She would sit on top of the refrigerator, and whatever man walked by without a cap or hat, she would rake across the top of their head. You notice, I said, men. I think she kept thinking about her prior owner, who had been so mean to her. The clawing was all before I had her declawed.

It got so bad with her surprise attacks she started even sitting under the dining table and grabbing the men and boys around the legs, followed by biting and scratching. This, of course, in the summer while cut off shorts were being worn.

To my surprise, Liz went into heat. I said to myself, no way, she has been spade, but it kept going — night after night.

I called our vet's office and asked if this was going to happen all the time, what could I do about it so I could get some sleep. The lady vet who was the older vet's daughter-in-law told me to "try" what she was getting ready to tell me. They had taught them an approach in vet school. She told me to take a Q-tip (as soon as she said Q-tip, a cold chill ran down my spine, and I started to get a bad feeling) and take some vaseline (another chill). Take the Q-tip and dip it in the vaseline and then place it in the right spot and move it around Liz's vagina to give Liz a "happy event."

I told our lady vet that she was joking. It was a good joke. So, now tell me what I need to do. She said, "I am not kidding. Sometimes this works." One thing I forgot to ask after she said the word "works" was how long does it work in stopping the screaming and howling?

I thought as I left the vet clinic, there is no way I am going to do that! They had to be kidding me and just testing me to see if I would do it. It sounded so kinky if you did this for your animals. I had done a lot of veterinary work for our animals on the farm, but never had I encountered anything like needing to help an animal have their "happy event."

I went home and hoped that the howling was over and would never be again. I went to bed at 10:00 p.m. and fell immediately asleep to be awakened promptly at midnight with the screaming by my head again and Liz's butt in my face! It was not over. I was so tired of a furry butt in my face. You have no idea. I put a pillow over my head. She kept taking her paw and pushing on my arm. She must be miserable. I lay there feeling guilty about her problem. I got up and put my bifocals on, walked into my bathroom, and started rummaging under the vanity for what else but Q-tips and vaseline.

I thought I better get Liz, but when I turned around, she was already at my feet rubbing against my legs. Oh, my goodness, I am becoming an animal pervert under the directions of my veterinarian. I took out a Q-tip and dipped it in the vaseline. I then got down on the floor as near Liz's viewpoint as possible. She was howling now at the top of her lungs. It reverberated in the bathroom. Did I tell her I just wanted sleep, and would she please cooperate with this crazy idea? Somehow I felt she was sleeping while I was at work and only doing this screaming routine when I was home.

I had the greasy Q-tip in my right hand and was crawling around and around the bathroom floor after Liz. It took about 12 laps around the bathroom, trying to get her cornered so I could try the Q-tip. But then I realized she was all black in that area, and with my bifocals, I could not see where I needed to place the Q-tip. Oh my goodness, now what. I took off my bifocals and started after her again. This time I had a flashlight in my other hand. That helped. I was close enough to Liz when I cornered her this time that I could see the target! I aimed with the Q-tip and bam I made contact with the desired area.

Liz tapped her feet fast, screamed at the top of her lungs, held her head as if she were having a seizure, and sticking her tongue out of her mouth like she was licking. Oh well, whatever floats her boat if it will stop that screaming and sticking her butt in my face. I wondered how long I needed to let her do this and if there was such as thing as too long and if it could kill her? She just kept on carrying on, trembling all over and still screaming, and then she started licking her lips faster. I wondered what that meant. Oh goodness, now what, I had never witnessed this, but maybe by it going on this long, she would go out of the heat, and it would all be over. I threw away the Q-tip and washed my hands with soap and water. She was washing herself up at that point. Hey, maybe this was going to work?!?!?! She did not ask for a cigarette, but maybe the cleaning up meant all was well.

I returned quietly to my bed and prayed this was all over. I was almost asleep when here Liz came screaming again, jumped up on the bed by my head, and here we went all over again. So much for the Q-tip. We were going to the vet AGAIN tomorrow.

Back to the veterinarian, we went early the next morning. Our vet explained to me that while Liz was forming in her mother's uterus that a piece of her ovary might have been attached somewhere else in her abdomen, therefore causing her to still go into heat.

I asked him, so, in this case, what can we do? He said you have two options. You can take her to the veterinarian school, where they will locate the other piece of the ovary and remove it, which will run you anywhere from $5,000 to $10,000. I just looked at him and said, so what is the second option, Mr. Vet

He told me I could give her birth control pills every time she went into heat.

I looked him in the eye and said, are you telling me that you knew this all along when I was crawling around in the floor with that stinking Q-tip chasing her at midnight last night? That was human cruelty pure and simple and did not count for the embarrassment.

I got the pills, paid my bill, and hot to trot Liz, and I went home. The very first thing that happened when we got home was Liz got herself a pill given to her. After about three hours, she started settling down. Who in the world would have thought it would have started to work that quick? Thank you, Lord, for all the blessings you bestow. I was looking for a good night's sleep that night! And Liz and I both slept soundly.

One day a couple of weeks later, my red-haired grandsons were at my home playing, and the oldest redhead came to me and said, "Dranny, how much do it cost for that mecine to keep Wiz from being mean? Cause I will take my own money and buy it. She is weally mean today." I had the medication; I did not know she had been attacking the boys! Shame on me. I am sure I will not get Grandmother of the Year Award this year.

The youngest redhead was the one that you had to watch. He was the daredevil, and he could scare you to death. He loved coming to our house because we lived on a dead-end road. No one could see us for miles around. He liked to go outside so he could pull his pants down and pee freely. Believe me, he did. One day while partaking of this privilege, he looked at his great-grandpa and pointed to his urine flying way up in the wind, and he said, "Look PawPaw, I am better than a WaterPark!"

Dad and I always fished a lot at a nearby Lake in his aluminum bass boat. Fishing was not a hobby to us; it was a passion. It set us on fire. Even a bad day fishing was excellent as long as he and I were out there on the lake and giving it an earnest try. One day we were up in a well known Creek when the clouds were looking pretty grim, and we looked at each other and said, "We need to head toward the boat dock." We started packing all of our gear up as fast as we could and getting it placed in the right spot because the waves were already back in the protected cove getting bad. Should we stay, or should we go? Hard decision.

We decided to make a break for it and no more than got out in the river channel when it started raining so hard it felt like nails piercing the skin. I was thinking to myself that I had never in my life felt rain like that. Dad and I squatted in the bottom of the boat. I noticed the boat was beginning to fill with water; it was raining faster than the sump pump in the boat could pump it out. That was not good. The boat could sink pretty quick if the rain did not let up, and my measly attempts at throwing water out with a solo cup were at best laughable. And then what happened when the boat was trying to sink?

The most significant hail I had ever seen in my life came pelting down by the buckets full. It was like what brimstone must be going to be like as described in Revelations; I am sure of it. It hurt so bad that everywhere it hit us, there was a new bruise. I can't explain it; it was the loudest sound I had ever heard, and it was utterly deafening. Just when you think it cannot get any worse and you ask yourself what next? NEVER THINK THAT!!!!! I promise you that it will get worse even though you are stupid enough not to be able to think of how much worse it could be.

About that time, as if God himself decided to show us there was something worse, he managed to show he had decided to throw a lightning bolt right down on the tree close to the edge of the water and next to the aluminum boat. It was racing through my head. How safe were we? Lightening this close hitting a tree, how far does the electricity run from the tree, through the ground, where we were touching the bank and then will the aluminum carry the electricity to us, and then fry us at once as we were standing in water up to our knees or would it be a quick boil hardening the blood in our veins. When you are 4' 10," up to your knees does not mean much, but in a boat, it is over the seats. Oh my goodness, we were in a Thunderstorm Hell! So glad Dad and I could experience this together. Some fathers and daughters go to father-daughter dances, but my Dad and I go to Thunderstorm Hell events made by God.

Again, I realize when you read some of my stories, you may think I am a little dramatic, but I am telling you, I was the one that lived through it and was 100% certain we were going to die that day. They were going to pull my short, fat body weighing even more because I was now saturated with water from the lake. I have no idea how long it lasted, but in my memory, it continued what seemed like more than a day! When we were able to look up, there were limbs, leaves, and trash of that "hell of destruction" lying everywhere.

We were drenched and speechless because we had lived through a storm of storms. It was a magnitude 10 out of 10 for all you meteorologists that do not care. Only the brave and robust could live through such. I got our solo cups and started slowly dipping out the water while Dad was trying his best to find out what was wrong with the sump pump, hard to do because where it was, it was full of water as well. After what seemed another eternity, I had enough water out, and the batteries were where they would start the boat, and we limped our way back to the boat ramp and the truck. It was quite some time before we had another desire to fish.

Another fishing trip at the Lake sticks in my mind like yesterday. We were fishing back in another Creek. It had always been known for its bluegill to bed up, and the fishing was great for the large male bluegills. We were trolling along quietly, and Gabby was even with us that day. She hardly ever came along, so I let her have the boat chair in the back, and I sat on the big cooler where we were putting fish. We were about to get to a shady spot when I looked up, and the biggest rattlesnake I had ever seen was coming toward the boat with his head up in a striking pose like he wanted to bite ME. I screamed like a little girl! I knew I was a goner because he had those evil snake eyes fixed on me. He was thinking of a great fat target baby - here I come. I was trying to scramble, and being such a clutz was falling all over the bottom of the boat. Gabby had climbed to the highest area of the boat. Dad, as calm as ever, had picked up a boat paddle so slowly, and as the snake reared back to strike "POW," the edge of the boat paddle came down on the snake's neck-breaking it.

The snake fell limp, and so did I. Dad picked his limp body up with the paddle, and we threw him in the cooler with the fish. Rattlesnake is excellent to eat if prepared right. It tastes somewhere between chicken and frog legs. Did you realize that they have stored in their mouth behind their fangs more fangs if the first ones get broken off!?? Since I was the one that had been sitting on the cooler all day, I sat back down on it, and we started fishing again. Forever in my mind, I will remember those days spent at the Lake fishing. We had fished about two more hours, and then all of a sudden, the cooler came alive, and I thought a kamoto dragon was coming out after me, and then I remembered the snake was in there. It must not be dead and regained consciousness. I could not believe it's strength!

I wanted off that cooler and out of that boat, but then my baby girl and Dad would be at risk! I must have looked pretty scared. Dad, again in his so calm voice, said, "It's just that rattlesnakes muscles contracting and relaxing. It is dead as it can be. I broke its neck." When you are the one with your not so tiny butt on top of the cooler and your legs by the cooler crack when that snake had a fit, you want to believe your Dad. After all, he has watched over you ever since you were a baby to make sure you were kept safe. It was different, it was like you could hear the heartbeat of that snake, and he was coming after someone for revenge!

The snake went on to be beautifully taxidermed. It was killed in self-defense by a brave man trying to get two girls to shut up and not scare the fish away! Behind it's set of fangs were ten more pairs! He measured five feet long. Still gives me the shivers when I think about it.

Before the new house where I live now was built, we lived in the family farm home where my Dad had grown up, one of my cousins had lived there and one of my Aunts; all at different times. One fall when it was getting chilly, almost cold, Dad noticed a tree that had rotted and fell over down by the ditch bank. At the same time, he heard a noise and saw all the honey bees milling around, but he could tell they were cold and not feeling their best.

He came back and told Gabby what he had found. They picked up a substantial white dishpan and took off for the broken honey bee tree. As they walked, Gpa told Gabby that the bees are not going to live through the winter since the tree broke because they are all going to freeze to death.

Gabby and Grandpa had both covered as much of their skin as possible to prevent stinging, but the pull of the taste of the wild honey was much higher than worrying about getting stung. They were grabbing the waxy honeycomb full of fresh honey that smelled so wonderful, and both of them were eating it by the handsful. It was still warm when you reached way up into the tree. The large white pan was overfull, and it was a wonder to behold for all those who loved fresh wild honey.

All of a sudden, Gabby turned a funny green and said she didn't want any more honey to eat. I said for now or forever. She said for now. I feel kinda sick. I asked her would it have anything to do with the fact that you have eaten almost a quart of the fresh honey? She said that it probably was that, and she could not even look at it right now. She had honey all over her coveralls, her hands, her gloves, in her long red hair. She was covered in fresh honey. But she had an experience that she will never forget her entire life.

Grandpa was behind her, and bees surrounded him. They knew who the real culprit was that had opened up their nice, warm home. They decided that he should be stung a few times to remind him not to come back, or he would get it worse the next time.

My son-in-law had a job that had a rotating shift, and when he came in late at night, he would sleep as long as he could then get up and take the boys to school. He was sleeping in bed one morning when the smallest curly-haired, freckled son walked into their bedroom. Bob and Gabby's bed was so tall that all Bob could see in his site of vision was from Bishop's nose up to the top of his little head.

His big brown eyes looked at his Dad full in the face and said softly, "Dad, Mom did not warm my pants this morning before she left, so I tookeded care of it for her. It will be okay now." Bob, with one eye open, looking at Bishop, said, "Oh really, how did you take care of it? Did you iron them yourself?" Bishop told his Daddy, "No, that heat thing in the family room that is real hot; I laid them on the top of it, and it is woking weally good, my pants are getting weally hot."

Bishop did not have to say anymore because, at that point, Bob had become airborne and was sprinting through the house to the family room like an ostrich. He got there just in time as Bishop's pants were so hot they felt like they were about to burst into flames. Bob said, "Bishop, we do not want to put clothes on that heater because it could catch the house on fire." Bishop said,

"But it was woking good getting them warm up like Mommy always warms thems up before I put them on."

Bobby and Bishop had both got sick at the same time. They were two years apart in age but yet they were so close, monkey see, monkey do. They even shared every illness they caught at school. They both got sick, and Bishop had thrown up quite a bit. It must have been pretty gross. Bobby went into where his Mommy was at getting ready for work and said, "Bishop frew up, but don't worry bout it cause I tooked care of it." Gabby went in to check on Bishop and found that the way Bobby had tooked care of it was by laying his piddow over it. Gross.

When my daughter came to tell me she was pregnant with my first grandson, I did not respond the way she had thought that I would, and it was because she had said to me that they were going to wait five years before they started a family. When she told me she was pregnant a year after they had married, I was not angry; all I said was, "I thought you were going to wait five years." I did not mean to upset her by any means; I did not. I was just shocked because she had been steadfast when she said that to me. However, I found out I did cause her to be upset, and I never meant to do that.

When she came to tell me she was pregnant with Bishop, my second grandson, she came to my office to tell me, but it was full of my staff as we were having a meeting. She said I will tell you about it later. I nodded my head. She went into the next office, called me and said, "I have been trying to tell you all day long, and you have been in one meeting after the other, so I decided to call you on your phone and tell you that you are going to be a grandma again." I asked her where she was at, told her I was sorry. I asked everyone in the meeting if we could reconvene later and opened the door to my daughter, who was grinning and excited about the baby she was going to have.

When she let me know she was pregnant with the third child, it was quite different. They had already decided that Bob was going to take one for the team and have a vasectomy. Well, not in enough time. During their vacation to a Theme Park for a week, it seemed they came home with a little souvenir that Gabby carried back in her belly. She told me she cried three days before she could tell anyone that she was even pregnant. She could not believe after ten years she was pregnant again! Bob and Gabby told me that no matter what happened, the baby's name was going to be Skipper. It would not change. Never believe that line from a couple that is already tired from two older boys and find out ten years later that they are having another child.

Bob had started to trace his genealogy and found his family was from a place in Germany. So they decided the new baby's name would be after that town but with the different pronunciation of Skipper. By the time Skipper arrived, he had many items embroidered with his new name all over them.

After Skipper was born, everyone agreed that God meant for them to have another child. It seemed that their family was truly complete with that little guy. He became the CEO of four homes, and he ruled everyone. Everyone loved him the more.

I think I have already mentioned somewhere in the book that my father and I are both clutzes and falling or doing something that is usually painful or a danger to our bodies all the time.

One evening after the evening meal, my mother called me and said, "I am looking out the kitchen window, and your Daddy is hanging upside down from the tractor by the hem of his pajamas." I said, "aren't you going out to help him because you are 32 feet from him, and I am about 200 feet away, and you will get to him much quicker. Do you know how long he has been hanging there?" Her reply, standing still at the kitchen window. "No, but he doesn't look like he is suffering."

By the time anyone got to him, two men had come to pick up something had found him, and they got him unhung from the tractor. I still have the blue pajama bottoms to remind me of that evening.

Gabby and her husband Bob adopted a Doberman Pincher named Petro. Petro had not had the happiest of home lives, and they were determined to give him the life he deserved. Petro had a bit of a problem, however. He had a little bit of separation anxiety. When the whole family would leave the house, his freakiness would go into overdrive, and when they came home, their large wrap around couch in the family room would have all the back cushions pulled off, and he would have pulled all the stuffing out of each one. He would be lying in the middle of all the stuffing like he did not know what happened because the couch must have blown up. Don't get me wrong; it was not always the couch, sometimes beside the sofa, he would add other expensive items. They tried to help him by buying him a brand name volleyball. It usually took him three days a ball to tear them apart. Petro is one of the biggest Dobermans I have ever seen.

One year while they were gone on vacation, Dad and I would

take turns driving the 15 miles and letting Petro out to play for about an hour in the yard and do his business while we were there. In the summer, I would usually water Gabby's flowers for her. I stayed busy while Petro stayed busy.

One vacation, they decided to take Petro to doggie daycare in a town about 15 miles away. Maybe he would be ok there. Gabby and Rob had left my Dad's phone number in the event something came up. Petro's second day there Dad got a phone call from Doggie Day Care. They told Dad he needed to come and pick up Petro because he could not stay there anymore. Dad asked if there had been any problems. They told Dad that Petro had destroyed his room and never stopped crying. They had his overnight bag packed and ready to go. Please come as soon as you can.

When Dad arrived, there was Petro's little overnight bag and a bill for damage of over $200 that dad needed to pay for right then. They let Petro out, and he almost knocked Dad down; he was so happy to see him. It seemed as if Petro was saying, "Grandpa take me home. I don't know these peoples, and my family is all gone." Dad told Petro it would be ok; he was there to take him home. Now what? Dad took him home to Gabby and Bob's address and said this is the best he could do. Dad and I went back to the morning and evening schedule, and Petro was so happy to see us each time.

One morning Dad called me from the back yard of Gabby's house and said, "I am worried about Petro." I asked what was wrong. He said, "Well, he has been hunched over trying to poop for over 15 minutes, and he is straining, and he is bleeding, and it is bright red blood coming from his butt. About 4-5 inches of it is hanging out of him. Disgusting. I asked Dad if he had been over close to Petro and took a close look at what was coming out. Dad said, "well, I had not wanted to do that, but I will if you think it is necessary."

When he got to where the process was taking place, he said, "Well if I didn't know any better, but it can't be possible, I would have to say it looks like a woman's high heel, but there is no way any woman would wear a shoe with a heel on it this high." I told him that Gabby did, and she had a favorite pair that were red and had about a five-six inch heel on them. About then, Dad said, "Well, I'll be, never in my life. That dog just pooped out a whole shoe!!! An entire red patent leather red shoe with a few bite marks on it. He sure is a happy dog now. Running around and playing." I told Dad, he better enjoys his life in the next few days because Gabby is going to kill him over that red shoe unless she comes home with one leg. They were her favorite dress shoes. That means he had to break into their bedroom and get her red stilettos and lay and chew on it and then eat the whole thing. I do not know what kept it from causing a blockage. I refused to tell her this while she was on vacation. She can wait and see it when she gets home. I think we will put it in a gallon zip lock and put it in her closet. It will be the best way for her to find out, and when she does find it say, "Oh yeah, we meant to tell you about that." Dad readily agreed with this plan.

Petro was bad for chasing people. He had no intention of hurting them. He wanted to be friends with everyone, and he did not like people walking on the street in front of their house. He would chase them to various places and usually corner them. He loved going to the groomers and loved Bob, giving him a manicure or holding his head in his lap. Petro loved Bob, and Bob loved him.

Every time Gabby would come home from work or somewhere else, and no one had been home all day, all the wrap around couch back pillows would be on the floor with the filling pulled out. Gabby would start mumbling and then get a little louder until she would look at Petro and tell him that the day he died, she was getting a new couch. Petro would sit and look at her like she was bragging on him as if he had done something beautiful.

One day while fishing at the lake, we were having a good day bluegill fishing. We were only paying attention to the process at hand, which was, of course, fishing. I finally turned around, and sure enough, the boat had filled almost full of water!!!! What in the world had happened? It was a fiberglass boat. We then realized someone had forgotten to put the plug in the boat before it was full of water. Again, there was a lot of dipping going on with solo cups. What in the world did folks do before there were solo cups?

We would have drowned, and our boat would have sunk. As we were dipping, Stupid One and Stupid Two finally came to realize they were getting nowhere because they had not blocked the hole where the plug was to be placed! Duh. We had to fill the hole quickly. As we dipped out a solo cup of water, in would come two solo cups more. We grabbed tackle boxes that were soaked and placed them up on the steering section of the boat, the only thing above water level. I envisioned the Titanic. We tried all kinds of items but finally came upon a styrofoam floater that was the perfect fit for the hole. Thank you, Jesus!

What a happy dance that brought on, and it is hard to happy dance in deep water. Then it was up to dipping again with solo cups. I had become quite good at dipping with solo cups. I, for one, appreciate that beautiful cup that the company had designed. When all the water was out of the boat, and we tried to find the plug for the boat, it was nowhere to be found, and to this day, no one knows what happened to it. When it was replaced, there were three bought, so we were never caught empty-handed again.

At twelve years old, Bishop was beginning to think about girls. Their dates were merely on the playground. So the last week of school, one year, they all got to go to the city park's playground for part of the day. On that day, one student was the preacher, and there were several 'couples' that got married. Bishop was one of them. He and his girlfriend took clover bloom stems and made their wedding rings. I happened to pick the boys up from school that day, and I had Skipper in his car seat in the back. Bishop told me he had gotten married that day.

I said, "Wow, married." Bishop went on to say there were several couples in his grade that got married that day. I asked him if they kissed to seal their vows. Bishop said they couldn't kiss because teachers were watching them, and that was not allowed. I asked him how long they had been dating, and he said they had dated most of the school year. Trying not to laugh, I also found out that their dating in fifth grade consisted only of playground dates.

When their family went on vacation that summer at the beach and came home, I asked the boys if they saw any cute chicks on the beach. Bobby's response was "a few." Bishop's was quite different, "Grandma, I told you I was married, so I don't look at other women anymore." I responded that he was right and I apologized that I had forgotten about that.

The next school year found both boys "dating" and "complaining." Bobby broke up with his girlfriend first, and Bishop was not long to follow behind him breaking up with his girlfriend. It seemed that Momma was the one they went to for advice on girls. Bobby's reasons for breaking up were several. Bishop was just tired of the dating scene, and it just cost too much to have a girlfriend. When you talked to them, they just wanted to tell you about their problems. DUH Bishop! We would not want you to get bored with listening to someone else's issues now, would we? Both boys were soon back to being single guys.

Bishop had one playground girlfriend who he said he had felt for some time that there was something not clicking, and he had found another playground girlfriend he was interested in. Bishop went to the new girl and asked her first if she would be interested in going steady with him on the playground, and she gladly accepted. That being accomplished, he knew he had to break the news to the 'other girl.' That part did not go over so well.

The school bell had rung, and everyone was going inside. Bishop was toward the back of the line and Bobby even further behind Bishop. The little girl that Bishop had broken up with came from out of nowhere with a tear-stained face and attacked Bishop. She shoved him to the sidewalk and started beating him, flailing him with both her fists. She then realized he had on a hoodie and grabbed the ties on it and was pulling them around his neck and pulling them so tight his face was turning blue. He said he could not breathe when she was choking him. She was on top of him, and he could not get up. And, just like it started, she stopped, got up, and walked into the school.

When this disturbing story was being told, I asked Bobby, "Did you witness this terrible event?" He said, "Yep, I saw all of it and that girl is strong, let me tell you!" I asked, "Why didn't you help your brother and pull her off of him and break up the fight." Bobby said, "He was doing ok during the fight." I gasped at this response. I looked at Bobby and replied, "How could he be ok if he was on the bottom, she sat on top of him so he could not move, and his face was blue." Bobby said, "His arms moved once in a while!" I have had the opportunity to watch older siblings with younger siblings, and I do not understand why they do not care for their younger brothers or sisters.

My daughter wanted a daughter so badly for their third child so that she would have a daughter to pal around with like her husband, and the boys hung out together.

I told her I have no idea why she needed a girl because I have never seen three boys, even the four-year-old with so much drama going on over girls. One is crying or about to cry over a different girl every day or asking about a girl or talking about dance, and should they ask a girl to the dance. Or if they can take a girl to a movie this weekend or not. How their hair looks and how much "Gorilla Snot" it takes to hold it in place just like they like. How much cologne they should wear so it is not too much and yet the girls can smell it. But, the strangest thing that I notice is their socks NEVER match. It may be a tall sock with just a footie. The socks may be different colors or of varying fabric just so long as they have some kind of sock on their feet. What gives with the stinkin socks nowadays? Am I missing something?

While Gabby was in her last year of high school and taking classes at college, all the animals at our home loved her, and usually, when she got home in the afternoon, they would come to the garage and greet her. This particular day was different. Our little Calie girl came up to Gabby, whining and crying, laid on her back and spread her legs apart. That was unusual for Calie, our little girl dog; she always met you standing up, ready for a petting, happy to see you. Gabby noticed something else strange, and she screamed for me to come out to the garage. I ran out, and she asked me if I saw anything different about Calie.

Calie was still there, whining and laying in the same position. But, I noticed from her female region, there was thick green drainage coming out at a fast pace. Gabby said, "What in the world has happened?" I told her I was not sure, but it looked like a "bad boy" dog got with her, overtook her, and raped her. It looked like he gave her a doggie transmitted disease. She had to go to the doctor as she must be in pain since she came to you like this to show you something was wrong.

Back to our favorite vet, we go. Sure enough, she did have an infection that went on up to the uterus. And there she also had some puppies that could not be saved because of this terrible infection. We asked the vet to please go ahead and do a hysterectomy at this point. Calie was a sick little dog, and she was a little spoiled before her recovery was all over. It is a shame that there are so few pain killers to give dogs and cats. You must be so careful giving pain killers for them, and most of them seem not to help that much.

It was not too long after Calie had healed well from her hysterectomy, doggie VD, and loss of her puppies and was doing so well that I had walked out on the front porch when Calie came screaming across the front yard from the Southwest part of the lawn. I mean, screaming! She ran up the front porch steps and threw herself against the front door that I thought she was going to body slam it open! I asked Calie what in the world was wrong, and she looked up at me, and it was plain to see she had been snake bit. Her little nose and face were so swollen. She had to be in so much pain that it pained me to look at her. It might make me late for work, but I could not leave this little girl who was so precious to everyone. We came back into the house, and I gave her some prednisone and pain meds for dogs and tried to make her comfortable before I left for work, and Dad said he would check on her during the day.

What a change by the time I got home from work. The swelling was all down; she wanted some petting; she was ready to eat something special, of course, and to go outside to do her business.

One night while it was still necessary to check in your deer at a check-in station we were on our way home, we noticed a little kitten sitting up on the side of the road. It seemed that the kitten needed a place to live. When my passenger got out to try to pick the kitten up, the kitten would walk a few steps ahead and sit down. When the passenger would catch up with the little kitten, it would walk away before she could be picked up, and she kept this little act up until she led my passenger back to ANOTHER kitten. It was a little smaller and looked weaker than the one who had led my passenger back to the small one. They were both picked up and taken back to the house. They were starving and could not eat enough. They were gulping so quickly I was worried it would make them sick. You could tell by looking at their little bellies they had to have worms.

The first one sitting on the side of the highway and looking like she was meowing, we named her Lucky Strike because she was lucky someone found her. The second one after we got to know her, we found she had slightly crossed eyes, and everywhere you found Lucky Strike, the solid gray kitten would be right behind her. They loved each other and were together constantly. Since the gray kitten was always behind Lucky Strike, we named her Shade.

Shade always had a problem with doors. She could never decide which side of any door she wanted to be on; therefore she would get on one side and you closed the door, then she would scratch, put her paw under the door, and cry until we opened the door and let her back on the first side. Then, poor Shade would start the same old thing all over again.

Shade seemed to be a praying cat. While a meal was being cooked, Shade would climb into a chair at the snack bar and place her two hands one over the other and sit there like she was praying until the meal was ready to serve.

If Shade would get in trouble for anything and you got down and shook your finger in her face, Lucky Strike would spring to her rescue and slap your hand for getting on to her sister. It was like she knew that her sister did not get enough oxygen at birth, and Shade needed some help getting around in this hard world. Lucky Strike was never far from Shade. They sure made a cute pair.

When I was sick, I must have breathed funny when I had bronchitis. It would only make sense. There were so many times I would wake up with Shade sitting on my chest and her nose right up under my nose like she was checking to see if I was still breathing. Whenever I was sick, I always told everyone I was in good hands because I had a house mortician who watched over me.

One night some of the step-grandchildren were spending the night, and it so happened that Bralyn and his stepbrother were sleeping in Mom and Dad's guest room. They were sleeping fine when during the night the most terrible noises broke out. Bralyn thought WW111 had broken out, and Thrasher thought Russia was invading us. When it first happened, they both tucked and rolled off the end of the bed and wound up flat on the floor. There was no more gunfire.

They wondered why it stopped. Great Grandpa wasn't getting up, that was weird, Great Grandma had not woke up, and no dogs were barking. What in the heck was going on? They were too scared to look out the window and down the road to see if tanks were coming this way. It was the only thing that could explain it. Finally, they turned on the overhead light and noticed the ceiling fan blades had come off while the ceiling fan was going full blast, and they had hit all kinds of stuff as the slung every direction. The strangest part was the closet wall where the boys were sleeping adjoined Great Grandpas closet wall, and he never heard ONE sound. ODD. Great Grandma took her hearing aids out, and she sure did not hear a thing. So tell me - what do you get when:

Five fan blades detach at the same time + all lights off + blades hitting mirrors, walls, objects on dressers and bureaus + the sounds of all hell breaking loose + two teenagers being scared out of their wits and wondering why great-grandpa and grandma never twitched an ear. = SCARY!!!!

Bishop was still in diapers, so PawPaw was changing the diapers. Some days he would tell Bishop when he changed him, "Bishop, why do you do this to Grandpa? It is just like trying to clean off axle grease?" Bishop was giggling when PawPaw would say that, laying there with that red curly hair and the cutest giggle you would ever hear.

There is one summer – that PaPa kept the boys by himself instead of them going to Day Care. They were all as happy as pigs in the sunshine.

Remember, the boys were as different as daylight and dark. Bobby was all serious, reserved, and worried about everything and his hair as straight as broom straw. Bishop, on the other hand, was all over the board. You never knew what he would do next, and you had to keep a closer eye on him. Bishop did not seem to be scared of anything. His hair all red curls, and they flew in the wind. He had not a worry in the world but laugh and have fun at that minute.

One afternoon when I got home from work, I thought I would give Dad a break, and I asked the boys if they wanted to go four wheelin'. Sure they did. The four-wheelers Dad had bought for them were for their size, both of them were identical, and when they started up, they sounded just like loud honey bees. I will also add here that the boys at that age both had speech impediments that quickly abated after a few years in speech therapy. Both of them called the four-wheelers "orefeelers."

I didn't bother to change clothes because it had been dry, and the field roads around the farm should be pretty dry. The boys were in hog heaven. If you took them orefeeling 50 times a day, you would have thought you had given them a water park for their back yard. They revved up their engines, and I got on the farm four-wheeler. A prayer that we would all make it back safely.

I told the boys that maybe it might be a good idea that grandma went in front in case of snakes or other critters. They were fine with that plan, and I went the same speed as they did.

We were doing great, stopping now and then to comment on a wildflower or a berry, what the crops were doing. They thought they were big stuff that day. I could see them growing right in front of me.

I looked ahead and noticed what a big mess lay in the road. I realized it was where the water irrigation pump had leaked, so there was water over the road, making it one big water hole mess. I turned around and told the boys. You must do what I do when we get to this water hole. Follow behind me exactly and stay in my tracks, and when you hit the water, go very fast till you get to the other side to the road. Do you understand? They were nodding their heads. I asked Bobby to repeat what I had said, and he verbalized it exactly. I thought that was pretty darned good for hearing instructions for one time. I asked Bishop if he fully understood. The helmet on his head bobbed up and down. Well, ok then, here we go. I told them to pay close attention and follow me; it was very important.

I gunned my engine, and I could hear the boys gunning their engines. We were going to do good with this. I could hear them coming behind me. HoooHaaaaa! I made it to the other side. Uhoh, I could not hear the little orfeelers. Not good. I slowly turned around in my seat and looked back, and they were both buried to the axles in the mud in the middle of that deep water hole.

Now I had to figure out how I was going to get them out of the mud hole with my work leather shoes and my off white work pants I was wearing. The mud in that mud hole was nasty, and it would never come out of my clothes. I took a deep breath and took off my leather shoes. I knew I could not roll my pants up as much as needed, so off came my pants and thank goodness my blouse covered up my underwear.

I waded off into that filthy mess. How disgusting and no telling how many strains of bacteria there was in that water. I told Bobby to start up his orfeeler, and I got hold of the handlebars. I then instructed him to give it all the gas he could as I pulled him through the rest of the mud hole. He did exactly as I told him. We made it to solid ground.

I went back in for Bishop, the feeling of that filthy stuff was NO better. It made me shudder to think of all the birds that had been in that water hole pooping and placing salmonella and no telling what other kinds of bird disease into that filth. I got to Bishop, and I said Bishop, you ready to go? He nodded, yes. I gave him the very same instructions as I did, Bobby.

I do not know the difference, and I probably never will, but when Bishop gave it the gas, there was a water flume that came over the top of the orfeeler and soaked me with that filthy muddy bacteria riddled water. I was going to die for sure. Neither boy seemed to have a drop on them. To top it all off, the mud had soured, and it made it more disgusting. We all got back on the road and made it back home to Mom and Dad's back yard.

Dad asked me what in the world happened to you? Where are your clothes and shoes? I couldn't talk. I had to get home and get the contamination off my body. My hair was even soaked. Bobby had an audience of Mom and Dad. He stood on the grand stage and said, "Bishop and I got stuckeded in a mud hole, and dranny had already made it frew. She had to take some of her clothes off so they would not get dirty. But when she pulled Bishop out, mud went all over her. So we comeded home. Dranny has not talkeded anymore.

Gpa said to the boys, "Well, how about we take you guys in for snack right quick?"

I went home and took the rest of my clothes off in the laundry room and threw them in the washing machine, and let them go through their first wash to see if it would get that soured mud smell out.

I went to take a shower to see if I could get that same smell off of me. It was in my hair the worst, I think. It took three coats of shampoo and two loofa scrubbings to get it off my skin. That had to be in my sinuses because I could keep smelling it.

Lesson learned that day. No more orfeeler rides around the farm unless we took another direction.

One afternoon when Gabby had stopped by to pick up the boys, Mom and I had prepared a meal, so Gabby did not have to prepare anything when she got home. Bob was working the night shift so he would get something at work. We had all eaten, and Bobby and Bishop had gone out to play. Lots of things to do on the farm. We were sitting around the snack bar talking when Bishop came in carrying a baseball bouncing it from hand to the other. He calmly and quietly walked in and said, "You might want to come to look at Bobby cause he is crying." We all looked at each other and shrugged our shoulders. One of the grandkids crying, that was nothing new. Bishop went back outside as slowly as he had walked out, not a care in the world.

In a few minutes, he came back in walking the same way and said, "You might want to go check on Bobby because he is still crying and says he has broken all his bones because he fell from the top of that willow tree next door." Gabby mowed all of us down who were in her way to get to her oldest baby boy. She met him at the corner of my house. The first thing I noticed was that he was walking. So those bones could not be broken. I saw no bones sticking from any area of his body. He was lifting his arms to wipe away his tears and all the snot that was running from his nose, telling his mother he had broken all his bones. I noticed under the willow tree that the fall had knocked off both of his tennis shoes. That had to be a hard fall! I asked him where were you in the tree when you fell? He pointed to the top. The willow tree is extremely tall as it had been there for years. Again he burst out crying and told his mother that he had broken all his bones and could not breathe well. A look of panic came across her face; she said, "Mom don't you think we should take him to

Urgent Care?" I told her maybe Urgent Care but not the ER, and I did not feel it mandated that in this case. I figure he just got the wind knocked out of him — poor little guy. And of course, in Southeast Missouri, there were always tornado warnings, and tonight was no different, and the skies looked terrible. Urgent Care told him he would be fine.

One afternoon when Gabby picked the boys up from Gma's and PaPa's, Bishop got buckled in his car seat and was quick to tell his mom that he had gotten in trouble from Gpa that day. That Gpa had smacked him on the butt with the yardstick. Bishop went on to tell her he had stayed in twoble all day and got a whoopin'. Then he told Gabby, "I wish we could find me a school where I can wearn to be good." He had been a firecracker all day long and into everything. Everything that could harm him, he made sure to mess with it. He had an itch that could not be scratched, I guess.

The two boys were more like Siamese twins than anything else. They both were so hard to potty train. With Bobby, he was four before he gave into it. I told him if he would start pooping on the potty all the time, I would take him on vacation, and we would go on a real train ride. We would also sleep on real train cars that had been turned into hotel rooms. He was ecstatic and bound to potty break himself. We would see.

Now, Bishop, we knew he would be an early potty boy. But he insisted on going in his diaper. He was still going in his diaper on the day of his third birthday. The day after his third birthday, he was staying with me, and I walked into the bathroom, and he was sitting up on the commode. I asked him what he was doing.

Bishop replied, "I'm pooping." I immediately felt like an idiot
and backed out of the room. Then I stood there a minute and
knocked on the door. I stuck my head in and asked him why he
would not use the commode to poop in yesterday. He replied, "I
WAS NOT FREE YET!" He meant three. Well, I should have
known that you had to wait for a special day to climb on that
great white throne to conduct the first big experiment. Forgive
me, oh, Great One.

It wound up we did take the long drive to ride the big
train. We had a ball, and the boys so loved the train. For some
reason at their ages at that time they were fascinated with trains.
They loved every second of the train ride, and it went pretty
far in the mountains. What they liked was staying in the old,
redesigned train cars to sleep.

Mom, Dad, Bishop, and I even went on a carriage ride
through town. Bishop waved at everyone. You would have
thought he was Master of Ceremonies in a real parade.

Bobby and Gma were fascinated with all the fish ponds,
were always buying stuff to feed the fish. They kept buying up
bread from the restaurant and feeding the fish. When the rest
of us came out for breakfast, we found them feeding the fish
like they were never going to be fed again. Bob said to them,
"Have you seen this big sign here that says PLEASE DO NOT
FEED THE FISH." Boy, did the two of them run for it? They
did not want to get caught doing anything improper. They left
us all standing there, wondering how much bread they had fed
the fish.

We all went to an attraction on that trip, and Gma is terrified of swinging bridges. She opted for this trip to not make a trip across the swinging bridge. The last time she visited the swinging bridge, she was found crawling on it, whimpering. Everything makes her dizzy. Even the pier at the island can make the beach house spin for at least three days. We warn her, and she acts as she has grown out of it, but I would say at the age of 83, it just ain't going to happen!!!

We had a cat named Crabby, who we had bought as a purebred Himalayan so we could breed her with another Himalayan for kittens to sell. They are beautiful cats and so hard to say no to them when you see them. Crabby was a refined housecat and often hid among Gabby's stuffed toys on her bed, looking just like one of the stuffed toys. The closest registered tomcat we could find as a sire in the area we had to drive almost an hour to get him to come to visit our little princess was a beautiful boy with allergies. The family had named him appropriately, "Booger." We picked up Booger and brought him to our house because Princess Crabby was in heat. Of all the screaming and carrying on you ever saw in your life. But Booger was not getting near her. He was scared of a screaming woman. Come on, no way. It went on for three days and nights. Finally, poor Booger looked like he was exhausted and had decided she was a nut, and I want nothing to do with her. I am not the man for her; PLEASE take me to my real home. We felt sorry for him, and that is exactly what we did.

Crabby had got to where she liked to go outside at times, so we decided to let her. She would come to the back door and meow, and we would let her come back into the 'domain' she felt she reigned over. One summer, while we were on a weekend getaway, Gma was watching after our dogs and cats. Crabby escaped, and grandma was not able to catch her. But, Crabby did Spray out three premature kittens while she was outside. All three kittens were cold and lifeless by the time gma found them, and she never found Crabby. We looked everywhere for her. It was a sad time for us as we never saw our Crabby cat again. I think she liked the wild type of man cat myself and was tired of living a refined life. I think the rogue talked her into running away with him and starting over under a new name. We will never know.

When Crabby lived with us, she was extremely smart. She had taught herself to retrieve and stand on her back feet for food and also to sit when told. She was probably one cat with the highest intelligence I had ever seen.

After my Dad's only brother passed away, we went to pick out his tombstone. While there, I told my parents they should go ahead and pick their head stone out, and then they would have what they wanted instead of me making a mess of it when the time came. They picked out a beautiful stone together.

After the tombstone had been made and placed in the cemetery, the next time Gabby came over for a visit, she drove over to the family cemetery to look at the stone. Bobby had a total meltdown. He was crying and sobbing, and she could not get him to stop. He said, "I knew it, I knew it. They did not get one big enough." Gabby said, "What do you mean not big enough?" He said they ain't no way you gonna stuff boff of them in that rock." No matter what she said, she could not convince that little boy of anything different. He knew everyone had goofed up, and it was going to be a mess.

I had a cat named Cotton, and he was a beautiful soft cat.
He was solid gray and looked like smoke. His hair was so very
soft and, therefore, the reason we named him Cotton. He had
been starving when we found his mother had abandoned him.
He was only about eight weeks old — just a little ball of grey
fuzz. I decided to give him some raw hamburger to eat. He was
eating it so fast and trying to keep all the other cats away (cats
which were not there) that he bit through his upper lip with his
"fang" tooth. He went nuts for sure. He was scratching as I tried
to get his lip off the tooth. How was I going to do this? There
was just no way by myself.

I was already bleeding all over like a sieve from this tiny
little kitten made of razor blades. Doggone it. Who would have
thought he could have done all that. By now, I was dripping
blood all over the house. Gabby was about four then, and she
looked at me and said, "He's going to die!" I reassured her he
would not die. We would drive to PawPaw Walter's, and he
could fix it. In my head, I was praying that he could do this, so I
would not be lying to my daughter. With all my experience with
animals in my life now, I know what I should have done, but at
the time, I was completely blank.

I got Gabby in the car, and at the time, there was no
restraining your child, but I still buckled her in and had Cotton
in a little cat carrier. I had called ahead to tell Mom and Dad
we were on our way with an emergency case. All the way there,
Gabby kept crying that Cotton was going to die, and she just
knew it. I asked her if she had prayed. Her voice shaking, she
started praying in earnest that God would help Cotton because
he was just a baby kitten, and he didn't know any better than
to eat his food fast. Please help PawPaw help him so that he
will live. We pulled into their driveway, and PawPaw met us at
the door. The first words out of Gabby's mouth to Dad were,
"PawPaw, if you don't fix him, he is going to die." I looked at
Dad and rolled my eyes. Drama, Drama, Drama! We had all got
used to our little Princesses ways.

Such drama; she was a pure actress at an early age. We went immediately to the surgery arena. (Dad's woodworking shop) There he lay Cotton on one of the tables under bright lights. He placed a towel over Cotton and had me hold him tight, especially his feet. I was trying to handle my job best I could. I did not want Dad's hands looking like mine. Then Dad pulled out his long nose pliers.

Inside I took a deep breath and thought 'no way.' Gabby had not taken her eyes off the surgery scene before her one time, her eyes as big as saucers. Grandpa got hold of Cotton's upper lip, and Cotton was screeching like a full-grown Tomcat and Grandpa pulled on it like he was stretching it until he could pull it down over Cotton's tooth. It was done. Cotton acted as nothing had ever happened. He started washing his paws and bathing himself. Gabby had whole new respect for her Grandpa. He could do everything. She never knew he was a surgeon until tonight. Cotton would LIVE!

One Sunday, when Bishop was about four during church choir service, we noticed everyone was looking toward the wall at the end of our pew and giggling. We all looked that direction, and to the east of the pews, there was Bishop and the pastors' daughter square dancing. I guess they thought the choir music was so good it was worth dancing to the rhythm. You got to express your joy to the Lord some way!

When my Dad's brother got too ill to stay at home by himself, he wanted to go to the same nursing home as his little girlfriend, who had suffered a severe stroke. His little girlfriend had a cat named Meow, and Meow needed a home. I brought her home to live with me. Meow was 31 years old and had ONE tooth. She would only eat one kind of cat food, and it had to be the shredded type. If it was not that she would turn her head and walk away. We would buy her cat food by the case. She was a precious little cat and showing her age. I do not know how she had lived on the busy Street all those years and never had been run over. She had to be smart to avoid all of that. I took her to the vet to make sure I was doing everything I should be doing for her. Our vet said she was a tough ole girl to be 31, and to be eating with one tooth, she still looked good. He said there was nothing he needed to do for her. As old as she was, she was immune to everything, so no shots were necessary.

I had bought a pair of peace doves, and I loved hearing them coo in the evening. It was beautifully soothing. I named them Bitsy and Chester and kept them in a large cast-iron round cage. I cannot tell you the why or how I name my pets; I am shocked myself sometimes when I have realized their names I have been stupid enough to bestow them. Actually, I am ashamed. It should have been Scarlett and Rhett. They fell truly in love, so in love, they wanted children. In my research, I quickly found out you had to get a special light and make sure they got only so many hours of this light a day and from a certain direction. It sounded a whole lot like a Q-tip and vaseline to me. Seriously? Maybe they would get over wanting children. What with working, feeding a 75-gallon aquarium of fish, taking care of wounded animals brought me, and so forth, maybe they should not have any kids. I had a metal nest hanging on the side of their cage, and it was pretty bad for a nest, and I tried to keep mowed grass and other clippings in there for them to make nesting material. Maybe if Bitsy sits in it now and then she would feel better. Bitsy needed an antidepressant. She had some blues when she wanted babies bad.

I got the dumbest idea (by far not the dumbest I had ever had, but we will not discuss that in this book) and partially robbed a mocking bird nest and brought the eggs in and put into the nest and I thought maybe this would make them happy. At first, it did. It took no time for Bitsy's weight to stomp the eggshells to pieces. There went that opportunity right out the front door. It was not a good idea.

I was sad, Bitsy was sad, and poor ole Chester did not know what to do about Bitsy being sad.

A couple of weeks went by, and one evening on my way to bed, I happened to notice that Bitsy was on her nest. She was sitting on her nest all the time. Had she laid an egg? I lifted her to see what was going on. What the heck? That was no dove egg. That was a bantam chicken egg!!!! That had to be my Mom's doing. Great; who did she think she was putting a banty chicken egg under my dove. What a mess I am going to have now. She is NOT the boss of my doves.

I picked up the phone and called. Dad answered the phone. I asked him if he knew about the banty egg under my dove. Slowly he said, "Yes, he knew," but he told me I had nothing to worry about because the nest was a metal strainer, and the dove had not put any lining in it and no way she could keep the egg warm enough to hatch it. Last time I ever believe him on anything animal husbandry wise! I looked up to him because my Dad knew everything. Today, I did not feel like luck was on my side.

Another couple of weeks went by, and I was up late working, and I thought I heard a 'cheap cheap.' I thought there is no way. I had to be hearing things. I went back to my paperwork, and a few minutes later, I heard another 'cheap cheap.' Ok, that is it, I have to get up and see what that noise is for sure this time. I walked over to the dove's cage, and Bitsy was standing up, looking between her legs.

Heck, I would have been looking between my legs too if

there was a noise coming from between my legs like that! Bitsy's mother had never told her anything about this part of birthin a chick. Lester did not know what to think of everything. He always tried to do whatever he could to make Bitsy happy, but he had no idea what was going on right now. Something must be wrong. Bitsy would NOT quit looking between her legs, and that is weird no matter how it comes out your mouth. Lester had NEVER seen Bitsy do anything like this before!

I started looking between Bitsy's legs and talking to Bitsy. I asked Bitsy what was going on in there in her basket between her legs. She would not take her eyes off the egg. Oh, there was another chirp, and all of a sudden, there was a hole in the side of the egg, a pretty good-sized hole at that; and then another cheap and another peck into the side of the egg. That little guy was busy, and it was a loudmouth. That did it; I don't care what time Mom and Dad went to bed; I don't care that it is almost 11:00 o'clock. I was calling my Mom and telling her what she had caused to happen. Thank you, Mother, one more job for me.

I picked up my phone, and Mom sleepily answered her phone at their house. I asked her if she had any idea why I might be calling her at this time of night when there was nothing wrong. No one was sick or bleeding.

She said she had no idea, but she was sleepy. I told her I was up, and she was going to be too because it was all her fault that I was up. She wanted to know how it was her fault that I was awake still. I gladly told her because of that stinkin egg under the dove is hatching. I could hear her sitting bolt right up, followed by "WHAT?" I said, "Yes, that egg you so laughingly placed under Bitsy is hatching. The one Dad said would never hatch. It is coming out tonight. I bet you are so happy, aren't you? Well, come on over, and you can sit with me." She said she thought she would wait till the next morning and come over and see what happened.

I asked her to please convey to my Father that he was very wrong about that egg that would not hatch.

I stayed up to watch the magic and finally out popped a beautiful red potato colored little chick. I was sure it had to be a rooster the way he was walking around. He was scratching at the bottom of the cage-like a new baby chick. Bitsy and Chester were standing by the little guy turning there head back and forth, looking at this little one. Like, what have we done, Bitsy? He seems a little big for a baby. He does not look like any other baby doves I have ever seen.

About then going with the way a dove feeds their babies, Bitsy made herself throw up, but the new hatchling could not figure out what in the world his mom was doing. Why did she spit on him? Gross! Disgusting!

Bitsy was not going to be discouraged again, got herself ready to throw up, and again took her beak and went to the side of the baby's mouth and pushed opened his little beak, and once she got it open, she threw up inside. Well what do you know; he got vomit in his mouth whether he wanted it or not. Be glad it wasn't Vick's Salve. Baby chick got the idea real quick. Wow, I had just witnessed a true miracle. Two different bird species that ate different at birth being retrained on eating because of a mother's undying love.

Tears came to my eyes as I watched. Bitsy did not stop. She kept feeding the baby until she felt like he had had enough. Being as Bitsy and Chester were used to sitting in a nest with their babies until they were big enough to fly did not know what to do with the new baby because they couldn't sit him in the nest. So, at night from then on, they sat with him on the floor of the cage. Bitsy with her right-wing over the baby and Chester with his left-wing over the baby all night long. Baby huddled between them like he was the happiest new child in the world. Things were under control for the moment, and I went to bed at two in the morning.

The next morning when I awoke for work, the first thing I did was checked on the new family. The baby was much brighter in color, and I decided he was the color of a red potato. His name shall be 'Tator.' He learned his name quickly. It was no time till his new great-grandparents next door came over to see what had happened. Chester and Bitsy were so proud of him and showing him off to whoever came to the cage to look at their new son. Bitsy and Tater had it all down now with Bitsy throwing up in Tater's mouth, and Tater gobbling it up as fast as he could. Who would have thought this could have happened. God's creatures are so unique.

As Tator grew, he got pickier with what he ate and started to want grain to eat off the floor and some small gravel and sand. Then he got tall enough that Bitsy could not get up to his mouth to throw up in it. Tator reached the adolescent age of a bantam rooster, and he was beautifully handsome.

Tator was a Clark Gable of Roosters. His feet were so large he walked all over Chester and Bitsy. He then got that adolescent smart mouth to mom and dad, and it was time to put him in his cage above his mom and dad, where they could still see him and hear him.

It wasn't long after that Tater tried to start to crow or attempt to crow. Quite amusing because it sounded nowhere like a crow, but it was still LOUD. It was also before my alarm went off in the morning. I am sure Bitsy and Chester were trying to figure out why Tater was making that noise. As the weeks went by, Tater grew to welcome anyone who came to the house. He was one happy Rooster, that is for sure.

Why not? He got rocked to sleep almost every night. One of his favorite things to be pampered by was by being rocked, the grandkids aggravated him to death, and he would play with them. He was one rotten rooster.

When Spring arrived, Tater had grown so large; he had to be placed with the hens outside in the large pen. His head was hitting the top of his cage, and he was hitting his bright red comb on the top of the cage.

Gma is the one who moved him out there (she thinks she is like a chicken boss of the some big chicken organization or something) and watched him to make sure the girls were okay from this new dangerous-looking pet bantam rooster who was used to being rocked to sleep every night.

That handsome little rooster was for sure beautiful and soon became a big hit with all the 'girls' in the hen pen. He was just a hottie, and no one could say any different. It did not take long for Tater to realize what his purpose was in that harem of beautiful hens.

His fame and beauty started to fade when later in the summer, however, Gma got hot under the collar when the hens started having so many feathers missing on their backs. When she figured out what the real cause was, then Tater got a talkin. I informed Mom that you could not change what is designed in nature! The chickens did not seem to mind what had happened to the feathers on their backs, so why was she so upset? Losing the feathers on their backs was worth it to the hens because they kept coming back for more! Ima saying let Mother Nature Reign.

Tater, once out in the chicken pen and palace, had become the king. His spurs had grown to be very long. Long enough, if we're not the person who had rocked him to sleep at night and the one who called him by name and babied him all his life, he might chase you and try to spur you. Gma started to fuss that she had to carry a stick with her to scare him away so he would not try to spur her.

I made an appointment with our vet (I told you we were over there all the time and that does not count my parents, daughter, or my aunt) and took my special little boy in to have his spurs cut back as far as they could be without harming my baby boy. I placed a note on top of his carrier, "Tater, my most Special Rooster, please take extra care of him, he is the baby, and he needs his spurs cut off as short as possible. He has made Gma very angry. If he does not stop this behavior, he has been threatened to be dumplings, which upsets me."

One summer, I had a pet Bantam chick, and surprisingly I cannot remember its name. I kept it in a birdcage and carried the cage everywhere I went. My cousin who was from the big city, came every summer to spend a week or two and visit with everyone. One summer night, she was spending the night with us when my mom banged on our bedroom door and told us to get up and get out to the car as there was a tornado headed our way. The reason they wanted us to get out of the house was that giant oak trees surrounded our home, and any could smash our house right in two.

My cousin, living in the city did not experience tornadoes as we did it seemed, looked bewildered, frightened, and scared out of her wits all at once asked me, "what do you wear to a tornado?" I told her we don't have time to change clothes. We need to get out now. It was not my first rodeo, but for sure, it was hers. She picked up the pet chicken, and I grabbed two cats, and we ran to the car parked in the tool shed/barn structure. Dad and my brother grabbed the house dog at the time, Sam and ran to the pickup truck. Dad led the way and drove out of the driveway and down the road to get away from trees, and we followed in the car. It was raining so hard we could not even crack a window. It was miserably hot in the car as we had no air conditioning in our vehicles back at that time. Some folks did, but not us; we were just too stinkin poor.

When the worst had passed, we all drove back into the shed and let the dogs out, the cats out, and carried the bird back in to try and get some sleep for the rest of the night. It was exciting to my cousin, but to our family, it was another night of interrupted sleep because of a possible twister.

For some reason, when my cousin was down every summer, it seemed something died that we had to bury. There was always an animal burial of some sort. She sure loved burying animals. It was like it was her favorite thing to do when she came to the country.

One afternoon one of our old cats came in barely able to walk up the driveway like she could not take another step. She had never been a friendly cat but would tolerate you petting her once in a great while. Well, she was panting like crazy and fell under the bush near the front steps. My cousin jumped up and said; I will get the shovel. I asked her why she needed the shovel. City Cousin replied that the cat was dying and we would need to bury her. I then had to disappoint her and tell her that the cat was only hot and had fell down there because she was so hot and tired. I showed her she was still breathing so we did not need to bury her yet.

Not long after that we had a large red sow have a huge litter of pigs, but she decided she did not want to feed them. That was not good for the piglets. The local vet was called, and he gave her a shot of what he called Motherly Love. It was a type of hormone shot that should have got her back in the mood to accept her babies.

She did accept them, and boy did they grow causing it to

not be long to castrate the male pigs. I could not wait to help. Anything to do with veterinarian work, I wanted to be in the middle of it. The only problem, I wanted the scalpel in my hands. Dad always got to do that part!

One day at lunch not long after the castrations, Dad brought to the house a baby pig that he said he thought had pneumonia. He wanted me to see if I could get it to pull through. If I could, she was mine! I was in "hog heaven" for sure. I fell in love with that little pig right then and there. She wanted to eat about every two hours and eat she did. I would have to change her hot water bottle about every two hours so she could stay warm, and yes, she did have pneumonia, no doubt. She had an odd cough. I made sure she got her antibiotic shots twice a day, and then I put what else but Vicks vapor rub on her chest and tied a red bandana around her chest as my folks did me.

I named that pig HoneyDew, and she thought she was a dog. She ate dog food with the dogs and chased cars. She thought she should be a house pig. My Mom put her foot down at that. But HoneyDew was more than happy to stand and look into the house and fuss because she could not get in with everyone else. She was a beautiful pig. We would play chase in the yard and go for walks. She loved the company of humans.

You know all the famous weighted quilts that are so popular now. The weight of them is supposed to help you feel more secure and help you sleep better. Sure they are. Back in the 1960s, my parents made a weighted quilt out of solid blue jeans. Both sides were old blue jeans, heavy blue jeans, and tacked together with red thread. That quilt was so heavy you could barely pick it up to lay it on the bed. It usually took two people to put it on the bed. You needed a furniture dolly to move it from room to room. You get my idea of how heavy this weighted quilt weighed.

Here is my theory on a weighted quilt from having a blue jean weighted quilt placed on me as a child. I was never scared once it was laid over me at night because if I did get scared, I could not move while under it because the thing weighed 2,000 pounds. You were weighted in place so you could not move. I noticed when I had bronchitis, which was about once or twice a month in the winter, they always laid the weighted quilt on me. I was sure my lungs were no longer going to be able to move up and down under the weighted quilt, and I would die under that bundle of death.

But, another added insult to the weighted quilt was when they brought in the hot toddy. Your parents told you that you must drink it as it would help you. Yes, it helped you gag and want to throw up. The drink consisted of some whiskey, lemon juice, coffee, and syrup or other sweeteners your parents approved. It was also used as a wash for calves when they had pneumonia. Only you had to put a garden hose down the calf to make sure the wash went into the right rumen and not the lungs. The hot toddy you had to drink left a nasty taste in your mouth, and you could smell it for days. You could not smell anything else but the hot toddy. It is of my opinion and mine alone that if you had to drink hot toddies as a child, you never wanted to drink whiskey when you got older.

Some kids were lucky enough to have their parents make them eat a large fingerful of Vicks salve if they coughed, wheezed, or started losing their voice. The secret to using the Vicks Salve was to let it melt slowly in your mouth and run down your throat. The miracle cure for sure. Ask any kid born in the 1930s or 1940s. They will tell you.

Now, do you think there have been any scientific studies done to see if any kid that had to eat Vicks Vapor rub as a kid has developed cancer from it? Of course not; it is still on the store shelves. Everyone is still making their kids eat it.

But, by golly, you can make sure talcum powder is getting a bad rap. They jumped on the bandwagon on good ole talcum powder made from a clay mineral silicate and mixed with cornstarch. Now you tell me what all the women were doing puttin that talcum powder that far in the yonder regions anyway?

Then there was the Vicks Vapor Rub rubdown on the sore throat and the chest, then the throat tied down with a bandana kerchief covered to the chin with the 2,000 pound weighted quilt. Once again, we are back to problems with breathing. When the 2,000-pound blue jeans weighted quilt is placed on you, they should also include an iron lung. Our family could not afford an iron lung so we had to take our chances.

Once the bandana kerchief is placed around your neck, one of your parents would look at you gravely and say, "DO NOT take that kerchief off yer neck or get uncovered tonight, or yer gonna die!" That scared you to death as a little kid. It always scared me anyway. First of all, what did 'die' mean. It must be really bad with the way their voices sounded. I for sure was not going to move all night long because I didn't want any of that dying stuff whatever it was. And how was I going to move with the weighted quilt laying on me?

If we only watch nature and the animals that live in nature, we will soon find they have personalities that match that of humans at times. It can be pretty funny if you watch it long enough. I remember one November day while sitting on my deer stand. I watched an argument that I believe went on almost all day long, and there was no doubt which one was the female and which was the male during this entire process that took place right in front of my eyes.

I honestly saw two red squirrels get a divorce in two trees right in front of me. It lasted for 3-4 hours, and I can promise you it was the wife that was doing the cursing and throwing the husband's items out of the hole in the tree to the East.

It all started inside the East tree, a loud squirrel fight. Who will ever know what the fight started over, but it escalated to the point that the husband ran out on the large limb in front of the hole in the tree. He cursed her back but not as loudly as she had seemed to scream at him. They even used their paws for pointing.

As the time dragged on during the day, the wife would throw nuts out of the tree to the ground, and he would stand on the ground and look at her and holler with what sounded like cursing again. Now and then, he would sneak up the tree and sneak some nuts out and run back down the tree and bury them when he did not think she was watching. The wife was busy burying nuts when she did not think he was watching her — both stopping and saying awful things to each other. At one point, a chipmunk ran out and started fussing at both of them as if to say shut-up I am trying to sleep. Soon to be ex-husband and ex-wife turned on the chipmunk and started screaming at him. Chipmunk decided he would go back under the leaves and shut up.

The soon to be ex-husband ran up the west tree about 50 feet from the wife's east tree and carried in his mouth what looked like a ton of nuts and dumped them in his new bachelor's apartment. He kept carrying his winter goods up to his apartment, but it was not clear where he was getting them all from to claim and carry them. He had been planning on leaving her for some time and hiding nuts so that she did not know about them. I wondered as I left that area if either of them would make it through the winter or if they would reconcile their differences if the winter got cold and bundle up to survive.

You may think I am kidding; you cannot make this kind of stuff up; but it happens here.

It was deer season, and Dad had gotten a deer, and one of the grandsons was helping him skin his deer out. While doing so, my dog Sony (a small dog about the size of a beagle but looked like a schnauzer) decided even with his electric collar on he would bust through the barrier to see what was going on over in that yard because it smelled good and everyone was there. When Sony arrived, he met up with all the bigger dogs on the farm who were already there and felt like it was their deer. They jumped on Sony and almost ripped his entire front arm off. Sony started running home to Momma, and my next to oldest grandson was right behind him running, telling me what had happened. I looked at how horrible the injury was, and knew there was nothing that could be done but take to the vet and hope for the best.

The vet told me that he was going to try and save the leg, but it was going to be touch and go as there was some tissue missing, and it was going to have to be pulled tight and stretched due to that problem. If he could not reattach a nerve in there and it had been damaged much, the leg may have to come off. Man, Sony, why did you have to jump in the middle of a group of dogs all four times your size? He could only do the best he could do. The vet kept him overnight and had me pick him up the next morning. For a few days, I had to carry him up and down the steps to take care of his business in the yard. After about a week he was better and could put weight on his leg. That was progress. The vet said he was going to have to take it easy and stay in the house for a couple of weeks until all his injuries were healed up.

After that healed, I noticed he was holding his mouth funny

all the time, and he would not eat or drink water. I opened his mouth and looked around and found nothing and then just on a hunch looked under his tongue to find a small but hard cockle burr type object that he had gotten lodged under his tongue deeply. That was another trip to the vet's office, and it called for more surgery.

It was about six months later that Sony Gump had three growths appear on and under his skin. They concerned me because they were not hard, and they were growing fast. To our vet again and showing him how many growths Sony had acquired in just the last six months. He said it was probably nothing, but there was one he was a little concerned about. Back under the knife for Sony. All the growths came back negative, and I was ever so grateful.

His sister, Cher Gump, with zero surgeries, was the tattletale of the two. She told everybody from the cats to Lydia Sue. She pitched a fit if she wanted outside and not to do business but to be nosey. She was scared to death of thunder, and that made the others scared of thunder. I usually wound up with three dogs and a cat on top of me when it thundered. She is the one who could tell time and knew exactly when it was 10:00 a.m. and 2:00 p.m. That is when they got their morning snack and afternoon snack. She was on the exact mark every time. She would take her paw and push me on the leg to remind me. I don't know if she took it upon herself or if the others told her to come and remind me. Cher told on the cat if he got on the counter. There was NOTHING she would not tattle about; she was the informer of the group.

One day after a terrible rainstorm went through, a tiny creature was found in under a grain bin. Well, I guess you could say it more like floated to the top. Its eyes were not even open, and it was so muddy you could not even tell what it was, but it was brought home and cleaned up gently with a Q-tip and warm water. What in the world? It was a very tiny baby skunk. Who would have thought it could have survived all of that water. Its mom was so busy getting the others to safety; she could not come back for him.

He was taken in and placed on a heating pad, started feeding him with a dropper, and then a tiny baby bottle, and he was nothing but a big spoiled mess. He thought I was his momma. We named him Spray. He never Sprayed because he never had a reason for it. All the dogs were scared of him even when he was little. Odd how they know what he is at such a young age. He was so much fun. He played like a kitten, and his favorite of all human foods was marshmallows. You could not fill him up on miniature marshmallows. He could put them away so fast that it was almost impossible to believe he had eaten it. He would lay on his back among the couch pillows and eat marshmallows and expect someone to rub his belly.

When Spray got large enough, we would take him out in the woods and teach him how to hunt for grubs and other things besides marshmallows. He was great at his technique and did not turn his nose up at any of what nature had to offer for skunk food. We did this quite often, and we would try to sneak away and get back to our house. Every stinkin time we thought we had made it back to the house and left him in the woods, we would get to our yard and were all out of breath, Spray would run past us! How did he do that? What were we going to do?

The first winter, he decided to hibernate in our basement; it was amongst some fabric I had in boxes down under some shelving. Sure enough, he came out in the spring, so happy to see everyone as if he had never been gone. Starving to death and wanting to eat and drink everything in sight.

The next summer, we doubled up on our efforts and worked harder than ever with getting Spray back to his natural habitat. Nothing was working. Finally, we started making marshmallow trails out to a shed behind our house, hoping he would want to start staying outside at night. Eventually, that did work. Then a trail was made of marshmallows towards the woods behind our house. It went pretty far, but he could still easily see the house. That worked! He released himself back to the wild, what we had wanted for him all along.

Spray took joy in every minute of his life with us. He could find a piece of thread on the floor and play with it forever and be as happy as a pig in the sunshine. He could be given a marshmallow, and it might as well have been a piece of gold to him, and he would love you forever. He loved to play chase with the grandkids, and anyone who would hold him was his instant best friend.

God had designed this creature so that he was so beautiful. Stunning, to be exact. His fur was the shiniest I had ever seen on any animal. His mouth looked like he was always grinning. His little beady eyes were always spot on, and he never missed anything; it was like he had the eyes of a fly. He always carried his tail so proudly.

When a skunk is thinking about spraying something, he will tap his back feet first, and then his little rectum area will turn as white as a cotton ball. You better be running and running fast at this point. Things are about to happen. For other animals, if they get it in their eyes, it is about like pepper spray to them. Skunks were built with a good defense system, and that is no doubt. I do not think there is anything in the animal kingdom that even likes to eat their flesh.

My Dad had been to a small town near here where my daughter and little family live. While on his way back home, he happened to see an old flatbed farm truck, and the cab was red. He said he felt like the Lord was telling him to stop and buy that old truck. When he got home with that old truck, Momma was about to pull his head off just like a chicken's for Sunday lunch. At times she can be pretty rough on Dad.

He said, "Now Momma, the Lord just told me to get this truck, and I don't know why, but I stopped and bought it." Mom stayed pretty mad for a few days and tried to get me mad. I was not going to get in the middle of that one. I am one that believes you should always listen to that still small voice of God.

Within a week, it started raining. It rained like the rains of Noah's day. It did some serious raining, I tell you.

The flood occurred here in Southeast Missouri as no other flood has ever been in my father's life or his father's life. It has been in the last eleven years, so about 2008. My father is 83, and if my grandfather were were still alive, he would have been over 100. This flood was of one that only God could orchestrate. Dad could take his riverboat and run down our county road and all over this part of the country that had never seen water!

On top of that, the local dam that had been built in the 1940s broke, and all the water gushed from the lake. Everyone in south part of the state had always been worried if this would happen. Well, folks there you have it. What most people did not realize was that the further south the water went, the more it spread it out. It washed away everything close to the dam.

That is what happens when you do not let nature take its course. Nature's way is always the best route. Leave it alone and let it be as nature had designed. For now, that is what has been done.

So I guess you are thinking about where the big red truck comes into play, aren't you? I don't blame you. I have made you wait long enough. That big red truck hauled our cars out to higher ground so we could take another non-flooded route to work each day. Driving to work was so unusual because it was like driving across a lake.

Every morning we would load up in Big Red as the truck became known. Mom and her lunch satchel and me with my work bag and lunch, and here we would go. The water was so deep that it would run inside the truck around our feet, and you had to hold your feet up to keep from getting them wet. Alongside Big Red swam, our chocolate and two yellow labs to higher ground. They had to swim quite a way to get to higher ground with Big Red. Every evening they swam back out with Dad to meet us and swam alongside Big Red.

What I do not understand about flooding is why do people look at a road and see that the floodwaters are ½ way up on the side of a home that everyone has evacuated, that you cannot see any of the road signs as they are all underwater and then think that it is ok to drive down that road. The next thing you know, their car is floating, and they are climbing out on top of their car, screaming for help. That takes a special kind of stupid in my book. Hahaha. No, I know you think that sounds like something I would do, but I did not do that one, but it did happen near my house.

The next year or the year before the flood, there came a four-inch ice storm. Also, a natural disaster that only God could design. We had small generators here at home, but we could only plug in one or two appliances at a time because of the size of the generator. We used kerosene lamps for our light, and I had to dig out a very old telephone (rotary) to be able to have contact with the outside world.

Outside it was total silence at night, and all you could hear was the falling of large trees that had stood for decades and the breaking of large limbs. It sounded like war, and there was nothing you could do about it. The noise never stopped, and it seemed like you could never go to sleep.

I was on Administrative call that week, and shockingly it was unusually calm.

It was normally a 45-minute drive into work that turned into a 2 ½ hour drive because all I could do was creep inch by inch. Everywhere you looked, there were electric poles broken like toothpicks and cars and trucks in the ditches. I met no one in my long drive to work.

I was so tense when I pulled into the parking lot that I could not believe I had made it.

I took my time getting out of my car, and as I went to stand up after opening the door all of a sudden, my feet slipped, and I slid under my car with only my head sticking out. What in the world have I done? As fat as I am, how did I get in this predicament? I guess the heat from the car engine melted the ice a little and made it like oil, so when I stood up, 'swoosh' under, I went. I was like a beached whale. I hollered help a few times, but who in their right mind was going to be outside in below zero degrees weather and be able to hear me out here. I was in a big mess. How would I get myself out of here?

After a few more minutes, I decided to try to pull myself out by the bottom edge of the car. Then I started moving my arms up and down on the ice like a snow angel to try and melt the ice a little more. Eventually, I could feel myself move some. I kept it up until I could drag myself on out from under my low lying car. I felt filthy. Like I needed a shower. Then I went to stand up. NO standing up. NO crawling. I looked like a beached whale moving across that parking lot. Belly crawling my way to the Entrance. When I finally made it to the stop sign, I grabbed it to pull myself up, and it was so covered with ice, I slid right back down the pole. You have got to be joking, I said to myself. So I belly crawled another 20 feet to clean concrete, and about that time, someone came out of the Entrance doors and asked if I needed help.

NOW, someone is asking me if I needed help. I smiled and said, no, everything is just fine. It is a great day. Little chilly. But I had made it to work safely.

Gabby stayed home with the boys at my house because they too had no electric yet, as their house was heated by electric. I came home my first day after sliding to work, and there Gabby was at my gas stove with a kerosene lantern sitting in the middle of four gas flames. My heart stopped, and I told her that could cause an explosion if left that way. She cried and said she could never have survived as a frontier woman.

She kept crying and said Bishop wants to pee every five minutes, so we have to go out and get more icicles off the house to melt so we can flush the commode. I hate this weather. She looked pretty rough. Her hair was not brushed; she was dressed in the old-time thermal underwear. I had no idea where in the world, she found them. She went on to say, "I am sick of all this cold and all of this ice. I just could not have lived in the olden days when they had to cook over a fireplace and wood floors with cracks in them. Then she had a meltdown, a complete meltdown at the kitchen stove. I told her this would be short-lived. (I hoped it would be; what did I know?) I had never seen this much ice in my life. I guess I just lied to her to keep her from having a nervous breakdown. Bobby and Bishop went on playing like everything was everyday fine.

In three days, Gabby and Bob's power was back on, and when Bob came to get her, she ran to the car! No goodbye, no, it has been fun; just ran like lions were chasing her.

For two or three years, Bishop stayed messed up because of that ice storm, and the lights only had to flicker, and Bishop would moan loudly and say, "Oh NO, the power is going off again!" It affected that boy for a long, long time. He is fourteen at the writing of this book, and he still is not right when the electric goes off.

It was a very long time after the year of the ice that Bishop would be seeing the Electric workers anywhere working, and he would holler out, "there are the Power Rangers."

One of the dogs that I brought home had come to the house of our family friend. The friend wanted to find a good home for her. She was a beagle/basset mix from looking at her but pure breed she was not. Our friend lived about three-four miles from us, and she wanted to find a good home for her because she was away from her own home visiting family members and taking care of other people so the 'new dog' would not have anyone around to take care of her. The dog needed someone soon because our neighbor was getting ready to leave on another trip out of state.

Dad told her that we would feed her every day while she was gone, and we did. Of course, it was a quick attachment on my part. There was one problem. I was sure that the next stray that God sent my way would be a 4 pound silky, something small I could pick up and carry comfortably. This dog easily weighed 25-30 pounds with all her ribs sticking out at least an inch and a half. Every day we went, the more she tugged at my heartstrings. The neighbor returned from her trip and said that someone she knew thought he might know someone who would take her in as their dog. When she told me the person's name, the hair on my neck stood up.

This dog had been treated so poorly in her life before now that she did not deserve to be going to someone else who may not spoil her like I was going to do. I stepped up to the challenge and said I would take "Lydia Sue," which I had been calling her; as the four-pound silkie that God had sent to me.

My grandson Bishop helped me get her in the bathtub that had two inches of water in it to bathe her. She was terrified! We both were wetter than she was when we got only partially finished. We finally gave up because the terror in her eyes was so vivid that I could not keep putting her through this at her new home.

The first night I found out a lot of things about my new girl. Dad and I had already figured out whoever had owned her first had abused her more than we would probably ever know. I learned that she could not take a drink of water without burping it right back up, all of it, and a lot at a time on me. Now and then, even now, she still has an issue with the same problem.

I found out that I would never be able to fill her up with dog food. She ate like she was starved and would never be full. We knew she had been consuming her food aggressively every time we fed her, and we fed her a LOT every evening. But I fed my dogs an excellent dog food that was very high in protein and had real meat in it, not a cereal generic dog food. I researched my dog foods to make sure that what they ate would prolong their lives and keep them healthy. She was still ravenous.

I found out that she had at one time been a house dog. Every time she needed to eliminate urine or bowel, she went to the door and told me. I have bells on cords on my front doorknob, and she would jingle them when she wanted out. She was starting to show she was a smart chick.

It took her a while to learn to share with the other two dogs. She did not know the meaning of share. She had understood the sense of hunger too many times, and share was not in her vocabulary.

I have French handles on several of my doors. Lydia soon learned how to open the doors in the house and to the outside. I don't mean she pushed them open; I said she pulled them open. If the doors were not locked with the deadbolts, she would open the doors and let all the dogs outside. Lydia believed in allowing Freedom to ring!

When I put her first leather collar on her, she acted so proudly! Lydia Sue was so happy that she could not stop licking me. It was as if she felt she belonged; that now, she was at her forever home and had been accepted. Her tail wagged all the time, and Lydia carried her head so high. She had a smile on her little face all the time.

I had to be careful how I picked up an object as she would flinch or dodge until she learned there would be no harm come her way in this house.

There was a ring around her neck that was raw, red, and blistered looking where no hair will probably ever grow again. It appeared that someone had kept her tied out all the time and that she was always pulling against it to try to get loose. It brings stinging tears to my eyes to think about what might have happened to her at their hands.

When we first visited her, we were sure that she had just had puppies as three of her breasts looked like they had been suckled, and it had not been long since she had delivered. Her lady parts seemed like they had just given birth as well.

I finally got the nerve up to take her to my groomer for them to give her a professional bath, have her nails trimmed and rounded, and just a good going over. I decided to take the other two dogs with her so she would not be frightened since she was familiar with them. She seemed fine. I explained to the groomer that she had been abused and seemed to be extremely afraid of water, so to expect anything when he started to bathe her.

I went back to pick all of them up, and he said, "You were right! She is terrified of the water!" But, he did give her a good bath, and she looked beautiful. We bragged on her, and she basked in the praises she got. Bless her heart.

Her separation anxiety when being away from me was not good. If I left for just a few minutes, she would sit at the door and cry. If I left for 1-2 hours, she would cry and sit by the door and get very upset. If I were gone longer than that, I would come home to a lot of doggy diarrhea and vomiting. That is how upset she would become when away from me. I want to take a minute and explain to you that this was not simple tiny dog diarrhea. It was like you were in a cow lot of diarrhea. It smelled so disgusting I was gagging the entire time. It took an entire roll of paper towels each time, an old dustpan, a trash bag, and me wearing hospital grade gloves and a face mask with perfume on the inside so I could stand it.

I take my dogs with me a lot of places I go to. They love riding in the car, and they have the sweetest manners. But wherever we go, Lydia places herself where she can keep watch on me all the time and make sure that I do not leave her.

Because of worrying about her separation anxieties, I waited too long to have her spayed, and she went into heat! NOT GOOD! She was in love immediately with any male dog, whether neutered or not. It just happened that Sony, my house dog who she lived with, had been neutered.

But, there was BoyScout, Mom, and Dad's yellow lab who had not been neutered but never showed any interest in any way toward sex of any kind. I am serious as a heart attack. When I say this, I am talking about at least eight years of celibacy. Maybe he had taken the vow of monkhood, and we never knew about it.

For some reason, Lydia piqued his interest, unfortunately. During 'her time,' they sneaked away together one day for six hours. I was worried. Dad and I went everywhere in the area around our corner of the world, looking for them and their tracks. No Lydia, no BoyScout anywhere to be found. We were getting worried because this was entirely out of nature for either of them, but then neither had ever been in love before like they were now, what can I say?

I slept in my office that night on the love seat. I was sure if Lydia showed up, she would come to the back door, and the motion light would come on, and I would see it when it did. Sure enough, at 9:30 p.m., she popped up on the sunroom porch, wagging her tail as if to say, "Hey, I am home!" I let her in and called my Mom. I let her know Lydia was home, and as if by magic, there was BoyScout. I let Mom know he was at my house. He would not leave the sunroom porch to go home. I had to lead him back to his home three feet at a time. He did not want to leave his one true love. It was sickening. BoyScout had had sex for the first time in his life, and it was better than leftover supper!!! He wanted some more of Lydia. She was the sweetest thing on this side of the Mississippi.

Oh, my goodness, who would have ever thought about this. My Mom was so sweet in the way she was coaxing BoyScout onto their back sun porch; that sweet little southern lady that was so worried about her yellow lab. Mom was so precious in her encouragement to him that the moment she got BoyScout inside the doorway, and it closed behind him; she started letting him have it about what a bad dog he had been to be gone so long from his loving home. She told him he could not get off the sunporch all the next day unless he were on a leash. Wow! Side note: did not happen! He got off the porch the next day without a leash first thing that morning.

The next morning I decided enough of this; I got busy and
prepared a shock collar for Lydia Sue just like Sony and Cher
wore. I do not like to hurt my dogs in any way, but the shock
collar is for sure the way to keep them from getting run over by
the mail carrier, UPS or Fed Ex or anyone else zooming down
our county road. It is a wireless fence system. Sony and Cher
learned after only one shock that when they heard the beeping
sound that they backed away from the beep and stayed within
the boundaries that kept them safe.

I put the collar on Lydia Sue, and I took her and Sony and
Cher outside for a walk. Everything was going great. BoyScout
walked up to Lydia, and they touched noses while watching me.
He started to lead her off, and I let him. They kept rubbing noses
and walking toward the boundary line. One more step and Lydia
stepped onto the boundary line! What a blood-curdling sound
she let out as she looked at BoyScout like she could bite a specific
part of his male anatomy off and began running toward the
sunporch door. I was still wrapped up in her leash, and she was
running so fast, like the cartoon characters you see on TV where
they are sprinting, and it looks like wheels on them instead of
legs. Her ears were flying in the air, and she was starting up the
steps. Oh NO, I can't climb steps the right way anymore, not
since my foot was crushed in a car wreck, she was dragging me
behind her. I was too stupid to unwrap my arm and hand from
the leash, and yet this 40 pounds/ oh, excuse me, my 4-pound
silkie was dragging me along the gravel path at 60 miles an hour,
and my short fat body was in no way keeping up with her. She
ran to the sunporch door and sat down. God in all His mercy
was watching over me, she was on the long leash, and it allowed
me to stop at the bottom of the steps. I could still step up on
them one at a time with my right foot first on each tread.

When Lydia came inside, she did not stop running. She ran
through the French doors into the dining room and into the
living room where she passed my Manx Linx cat "Crabby," the
Q-tip cat who had a strong distaste for anything but herself.

When Lydia went past her, Crabby tore into her and smacked her like crazy. Crabby has no claws. Lydia does not know that; Lydia only knows that she is a cat, and cats hurt you, and when they strike at you, it can be painful. Lydia had gone through two unpleasant experiences in a matter of five minutes, and she needed to lay down and lick her wounds. She climbed onto the couch, and there she stayed until 6:30 a.m. the next morning.

At 6:30, I let Lydia out as I did Sony and Cher. There was BoyScout at the back door waiting for his one true love. They watched me watch them, and they wandered off around the corner of the house where I could not see them. I think that it is strange that they knew what they were doing was not favored by their masters.

It did not take long, Lydia let out another blood-curdling howl and came running back to the sunroom porch again! I did not witness the encounter, but for the amount of time she howled I am sure she had been, let's say under the desires of BoyScout and was trying to get untangled from him, and I think he was getting some shock as well. Back in the house, she came. I am sure she was confused about what was happening? The six hours of frolic away from home two days ago had been nothing like this! When he had shared his love, it had not felt like this before. This time it was like Satan's pitchfork handle being placed into her alley of love. For the mercy of God, what had happened to that dog who was so much fun the other day?

I waited a couple of hours after the dogs had eaten their breakfast and let them out again. BoyScout was sitting at the back door like a dying calf in a hailstorm. I had NEVER seen a dog look this sad before. Lydia looked at him longingly, but she refused to go out that door. She went to the front door of the house. I let all the dogs out the front door. In a matter of two minutes, here comes BoyScout around the corner of the house towards Lydia. Lydia took off, running toward the back door of the house. I went to the back door of the house to see what was happening. Lydia was sitting on the porch with her back against the door and acting like she did not know BoyScout.

BoyScout was looking very confused and hurt. He could not imagine what had happened to his fun-loving girlfriend, who had frolicked with him just two days before for six blissful hours. He was depressed! Ruby was frightened forever! I think that her "time of estrous" was about over. It was about time to call my vet and get this surgery over.

When my daughter and her husband had to go out of town on a business trip, they asked if I would stay with their two oldest boys, and the four-year-old would stay with our Aunt. The security alarm for their security system awakened me about 2:00 a.m. right by my side of the bed. I stumbled into the kitchen, and there I met Bobby ever so tall at 15 years old, and I asked him what was going on that set off the security alarm.

Nonchalantly he said he had forgotten to turn the alarm off while he went out to the storage room where the big freezer was to get some ice cream. But he had punched some buttons, and the alarm was off, and all was good. He had called his mom, so she knew what was going on, and all was good grandma. That did not put me at peace for some reason. My gut wanted to call my daughter, but I know they needed sleep.

Bob's phone happened to be on vibrate, and Gabby had set her's to sleep mode, so when the first call came from the cops, neither of them had heard their phones. By the time the second call came through, the house I was in had been surrounded by cops and the SWAT team, and they were ready to burst through the ten-foot living room window. Gabby woke Bob and said there is trouble at home, and you better answer your phone as the SWAT team is wanting to break through our living room windows. They asked Bob if they had his permission to go ahead with the planned mission. The intruders were identified in the kitchen area of the home.

Bob told them to wait one second so he could check his security camera system at home, and he saw the two suspects they were talking about, and it was Bobby and I. Bobby had gone to the freezer for food. Because the security system alarm was so loud, Bobby and I had rendezvoused in the kitchen. Still unknown to Bobby and I, Bob told the SWAT team to back down and not burst into his home that the intruders were his son and mother-in-law.

Bob and Gabby then talked to Bobby to find out what he had done wrong with the alarm system. He had pushed the wrong button to gain entrance to where the ice cream was being held hostage in the freezer.

By then, I noticed there were a LOT of blue and white bright flashing lights out in the street through the curtain sheers and blind slats and was feeling sorry for whoever must have been in a wreck. At that time, I did not know the SWAT team surrounded us.

I had said that I would never have another cat, when my 21-year-old blind cat Cimaron that our daughter left when she moved out, and my Manx Lynx cat Crabby passed on to cat heaven. I was getting too old to deal with all the cat hair and the litter pan. Again I say, God has a sense of humor. He sent me a tiny, skinny, starving black and white kitten with the most beautiful markings that anyone would fall in love with instantly. He ran to my parents while they were working in the garden, crying. Mom and Dad said it sounded like he said, "Help Me!

Help Me!" They scooped him up and took him inside, and he ate and ate and ate. He was so very tiny and was not even old enough to be weaned from his mother.

Things went along famously UNTIL he found out what his front claws were for, and he clawed on every piece of leather furniture that I owned. I could not believe it! How quickly he managed to scratch up so much! He shredded, I mean destroyed the top of a new footstool I had recovered, and I did not have enough of the fabric left to have it redone again. I hated to declaw, but there was no way around it. If he was going to live here, it had to happen. He had a tall cat tree, but hey, why scratch on that when you could scratch on leather?

I named him Scorch, because of the beautiful markings on his face that looked like he had two mustaches under his cute little nose. Even when I took him to the vet, they all commented on how different he was marked up. They said that they see so many kittens and cats, but they rarely had one come in that is marked up extraordinarily like this. I told them that the Lord sure used His finger paints on this one. I couldn't turn him down when he showed up next door.

He recovered fantastically from the surgery as the vet said he would since I was having it done at four months of age. Now we had to wait two more months to have him neutered. I am pro for neutering and spaying any abused animal I bring into my home.

At the vet's office, and I am there a lot, they all know me by my first name. I think they dread me at times, wondering what I am bringing in to them. While I was there, I talked to the young vet, the older vet's son, who had also decided to be a veterinarian as well as his wife. We love the whole family. They are good people, loved their family, and they had worked hard for a living. They were kind to my pets. They knew how I loved my pets.

I told the young vet about my Lydia and that I needed to have her spayed, but she was in heat right now. I knew it was bad to have her spayed right now due to problems with bleeding. But as soon as she was over her heat, I would arrange for the spay. But there was one problem. Her separation anxiety is worse than any animal I have ever owned in my entire life. I asked him how we could handle it when I brought her in for surgery; otherwise, there would be diarrhea and vomiting everywhere for them to clean up.

He told me as soon as I brought her in, they would give her a pre-op sedative so she would not know I was leaving. Then she would be under anesthesia during surgery, and they would have me come pick her up before she was out of anesthesia, and she would not know that I had ever left her. I told him that it was a deal. I did not want to have Lydia go through anything traumatic, nor did I want to cause them a lot of extra work.

My bright idea backfired! On Tuesday morning, Lydia went out, and I thought everything would be ok. Not to be! BoyScout came over when I went back into the house for a minute and raped my baby girl, who was no longer interested. Lydia was so upset, trying to get up the steps to the front door, but she was **dragging** BoyScout up the five steps best she could by his most special purpose that hangs below his belly that now was turned backward between his legs was over twice her size, and she could not get detached from him!

I felt so sorry for Lydia. I tried spraying cold water on BoyScout's man tools, I scolded him, I told him what pond scum he had become and nothing worked. When he got away, she came in and threw up by the back door in the sunroom and had stress diarrhea in 20 spots in the same room! BoyScout, look what you have caused now. Mercy sakes!

All I could do was clean and steam mop for an hour after the roll of paper towels and a trash bag. It was crazy! My poor little girl dog. She did not deserve this. When this heat is over, and she has her surgery, if he keeps this up, he will be neutered or have transgender surgery, something I have not asked my vet to do for me yet, but it is coming, and no, I do not feel bad about it.

He tried to get back on my good side this afternoon by wagging his tail and smiling. I told him that it was not going to happen anytime soon and to stay away from my house and my Lydia.

I will not make any bones about it; our family is no different than any other family except we take each day at a time, and we try to live every moment as if it were our last. It allows us all to laugh a lot, and to laugh; we must admit it makes the world go around a little bit easier.

All of us are blessed so abundantly, and we all take so many things for granted that God allows us to enjoy every day. There may be things wrong in the world, but what a better place to improve than starting with ourselves.

Printed in the United States
By Bookmasters